Rejected, But Accepted By HIM

By DR. YOLANDA WEBSTER

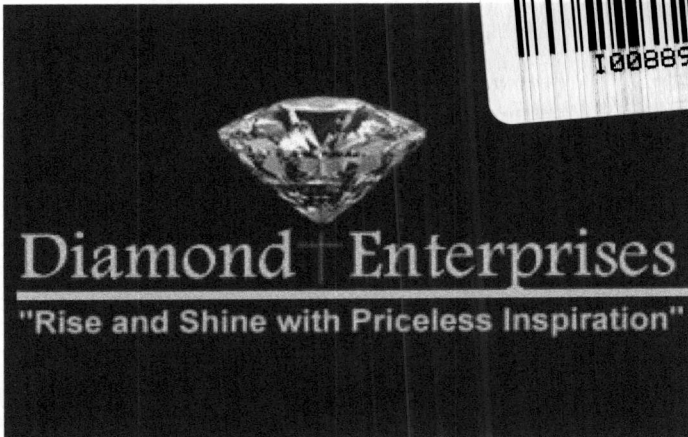

Diamond Enterprises
"Rise and Shine with Priceless Inspiration"

Contents

Acknowledgements

My deepest appreciation to...

Gregory. Thanks for being my husband, best friend, most faithful supporter, co-laborer in raising the family, father of our children, and lover. You are truly God's gift to me, and I value and treasure you. I honor you, Gerald.

Our five children, Ramothea, Tashonna, Damien, Parris, and Raquan. All of you have brought great joy to my life. You are each a special treasure to me. Thank you for sharing in the call of God and encouraging me to write. I love spending time with each of you.

Ann Marie and Jerry Mallory, thanks for your diligence and patience in working with me. I thank you tremendously for your support. You have been indispensable to me for many years now as both friend and encourager.

Lois Rochford, many thanks for constant encouragement and exceptional friendship through many years of friendship.

Lavonne Burno, thank you for being a big sister, and friend throughout so many years, and special appreciation for being there.

Kevin and Qwendolyn Joseph, a special thank you for the love, the laughter and the prayers. I thank you from the bottom of my heart.

Jacqueline George, thank you for your friendship and support for many years.

Mattie Moultrie Wilson, thank you for your love, encouragement and prayers as you watched me grow into womanhood.

Most important, my sincere appreciation to my Lord, Jesus Christ. There are no words that can adequately acknowledge all You have done for me and for Your people. I love You more than I am able to convey.

FOREWORD

Yolanda Webster's book Rejected, but Accepted by HIM paints a story of rejection on the canvas of Jesus Christ's life. Reading about rejection opens and challenges your mind while including you and causing you not to be captivated by the offense taken place in the very word of rejection.

Rejection is so deep and so vast it's like a tree with many roots.

You will learn about yourself and how the mind works. You will be informed about the human spirit and you will know what God's word says about rejection.

Her book dives off the despair of unrealistic expectations into the essence of reality. She is able to squeeze the truth out of you without physical touch. After reading her book you would have received a life changing experience.

Her views pass the borders in the lives of people and reaches into the heart of the reader. You would not be able to put this book down. You will find yourself telling your family, friends, co-workers, classmates and church family about this book so they can be elevated and enlightened as you were.

This book will build character and courage in you. It will reach from the youngest to the oldest. No one is left out. You will be faced with truth that will cause you to make a decision to change your life. The difference with this book from other books, you will be able to carry it through the entire chapters of your life and still find areas to repair, strengthen and pass on to others.

This author just doesn't inform you. This author shows you how to obtain and maintain a greater life. You will find yourself dreaming and having visions while reading this book.

If low self esteem has crippled your mind and stagnated your steps and held up your potential read what this author wrote. It will empower you to bring your head above water and strive on a higher plateau while you take into your heart what's written therein.

The cement of the word of God is poured out in front of you so you can stand and live on solid good ground.

In this book you will find that you have a date with destiny which was orchestrated by God before the world began. Therefore you will find out you cannot lose because the winners path is right in front of you and in your hands. This book will change your present and future which cannot be controlled by yesterday's situations.

While this book builds a curriculum for a better life in your spirit, mind, and body, you will also be inspired, encouraged and challenged.

Proverbs 4:7 (KJV)

Wisdom [is] the principal thing; [therefore] get wisdom: and with all thy getting get understanding.

Read it, receive it, enjoy it and live it.

-Pastor Jerry S. Mallory, Senior Pastor of Kingdom Life Builders Int'l Ministries Valrico, Florida

Introduction

Rejection is a difficult topic to talk about for most people, including myself. No one wants to admit that they did not measure up in some way, true or false, to another's expectations. Sometimes people get rejected for good reasons and sometimes they get rejected for bad reasons, but either way, rejection hurts. Every human being gets rejected at some point or another, and most people get rejected many times, whether it be from a romantic interest, a job, an apartment application or a friend. I think that just realizing the fact that everyone gets rejected sometimes make it easier to deal with - if you have a friend who rejects you, it helps to understand that most people who have friends has experienced one rejecting them. You are not alone in this.

One of the most interesting things about rejection is the fact that it is so difficult to admit even to yourself. When a boyfriend dumps you, you don't even want to think of it that way, much less acknowledge to anyone else. Think about it: the last time you were rejected by someone you cared about did you really admit it and the reasons why even to yourself? Rejection is much easier to admit when you have an easy reason to assign to it that doesnt make you do any soul searching. If you didn't get that job, you may say, "they needed someone with more experience." Rarely will you even think "I did not have the ability to do that job," even if that is the case. This has both positive and negative effects: positive because it makes it easier to maintain your confidence, negative because it does not allow for reflection on your faults and how they might be fixed.

People react to rejection with a variety of negative emotions from despair and withdrawal to frustration and intense anger. Each in America, over a million people are stalked, almost always by ex-boyfriends, ex-husbands or ex-lived-in partners. Something that really jolted me was that 80% of these people are actually attacked physically by their stalker. Why do people stalk? People who stalk are those who are not mature enough to deal with the negative emotions of rejection, usually because they refuse to acknowledge that rejection and the physical pain that comes with it even to themselves. Denial is a powerful and very dangerous mental tool.

One of the best signs of a mature person is how they react to rejection. Rejection is an emotional[y, mentally and physically painful experience. I think most people who have been rejected by someone they have had a long term romantic relationship with would prefer the pain of a broken bone to the pain of a broken heart. I know I would. But that is not an option. It is very important when dealing with rejection to first acknowledge it to yourself and then to people close to you. Don't tell the world, but it is good to talk about it with those you trust. Pick yourself up and move on with your life. Don't give up or quit, get back in the game (whatever that game is = job hunting, romantic etc.) and try again.

Social rejection occurs when an individual is deliberately excluded from a social relationship or social interaction. The subject matter includes both interpersonal rejection (or peer rejection) and romantic rejection. A person can be rejected on an individual basis or by an entire group of people. Additionally, rejection can be either active, by bullying, teasing, or ridiculing, or passive, by ignoring a person, or giving the "silent treatment." The experience of being rejected is personal for the recipient, and it can be discerned when it is not actually present. The word "excommunication" is often used for the process.

Although humans are social beings, some level of rejection is an inevitable part of life. Nonetheless, rejection can become a problem when it is prolonged or consistent, when the relationship is important, or when the individual is highly sensitive to rejection. Rejection by an entire group of people can have especially negative effects, particularly when it results in social isolation.

The experience of rejection can lead to a number of adverse psychological consequences such as loneliness, low self-esteem, aggression, and depression. It can also lead to feelings of insecurity and a heightened sensitivity to future rejection.

Rejection is emotionally painful because of the social nature of human beings and our basic need to be accepted in groups. According to Abraham Maslow and other theorists have implied that the need for love and belongingness is an essential human motivation. Furthermore, all humans, even introverts, need to be able to give and receive affection to be psychologically healthy.

Mental health practitioners believe that simple contact or social interaction with others is not enough to fulfill this need. Instead, people have a strong motivational drive to form and maintain caring interpersonal relationships. People require both stable relationships and satisfying interactions with the people in those relationships. If one of the two ingredients is missing, people will begin to feel lonely and unhappy. Therefore, rejection is a significant threat. In fact, the majority of human anxieties appear to echo concerns over social exclusion.

Being a member of a group is also important for social identity, which is a key element of the self-concept. The main purpose of self-esteem is to observe social relations and notice social rejection. In this view, self-esteem is a measurement which activates negative emotions when signs of exclusion appear.

Realistically, life is full of various rejections and how you deal with it defines who you are. Can you pick yourself up and move on? Are you willing to try again? Can you keep up a good attitude even in the face of rejection?

Laughter is a great cure for rejection. The ability to laugh at yourself and your situation is a key to making that situation much, much easier to deal with. Remember Psalms 34:18 that The Lord is close to the brokenhearted and saves those who are crushed in spirit. God has said "Never will I leave you, never will I forsake you." So we say with confidence, "The Lord is my helper, I will not be afraid. What can man do to me?

God is at work in our lives even when we can't see Him. He knows the ending of everyone's story before the beginning. We must learn not to trust what we can see and feel, but put our trust in God and His Word. Never mistrust the presence and activity of God in our lives. God has more supernatural soldiers fighting for us than Satan has fighting against us. He permits these seasons to strengthen us as we learn to depend on Him.

Chapter One: Rejection

An All-Too-Familiar Experience

To reject someone means to refuse to grant that person recognition or acceptance, to discard that individual as being worthless. Have you ever felt rejected?

- Did you feel rejected because your father withdrawn and cold, too active to give you time and attention?
- Did you feel rejected because your mother preferred your older sister who was cuter or brighter?
- Did you feel rejected because you were not skilled in athletics and when the class divided up into groups, you were the last one picked?
- Did you feel rejected because your school clothes were not as appealing as the other kids' and they made fun of you?
- Were you overweight? Were you unattractive? Did you have pimples? Did you have to wear thick glasses?
- Did you lose your job because you were getting older?

- Did you date a man for numerous years, anticipating to marry him, only to have him walk away?
- Do you feel rejected by your children, after giving your life to raise them and to provide for them the benefits you didn't have?
- Did your husband leave you in midlife for another woman-or worse yet, another man?

Rejection is a painful experience no matter what the cause, and all too often we don't ascribe enough blame to the rejecter. We simply accept his or her evaluation of us and carry a feeling of inferiority or of being "damaged goods" all our lives.

Rejection Is Not a Measure of True Worth

But does rejection really influence our key worth? If individuals don't respect me as a total person because they don't like my looks or my performance, does that mean I really am what they think I am? Am I innately less valuable? Should I permit them to stereotype me for the rest of my life? What if they are incorrect? They usually are.

Let us consider Jacobs two wives, Leah and Rachel. In Genesis 30, we learned how envy and jealousy can destroy harmony and love in a family. As we examine the emotional obstacle of rejection, let's take a closer look at Leah's spiritual voyage, because Leah was a woman who lived with the pain of rejection every day of her life.

First of all, Leah was never regarded with high honor by her husband. In that day, it was the father's responsibility to arrange for his daughters to marry. During the seven years Jacob worked for Rachel, Laban could have attempted to find a husband for Leah. If he had offered a big-enough dowry, he would have found someone to marry her. Obviously, he thought she was hopeless as a marriage prospect and the only way to get rid of her was to impose her on poor Jacob, who was overwhelmed with love for Rachel. Laban slipped Leah off to Jacob like a deceitful business man getting rid of damaged goods at full cost.

Leah: Unwanted and Unloved

Can you picture how Leah must have shrink when Jacob looked at her in the morning light with surprise, disgust and rage? That terrible deception on Jacob's wedding night set in motion much of the sadness that the family experienced for decades to come. Sadly, Leah didn't deserve that rejection. Obviously, her rejection was derived on her looks-her weak eyes. Nobody regarded her character, her inner self, or her mind. This isn't much different than the way things are today. You've never seen an unattractive Miss America, have you?

"Jacob loved Rachel more than Leah." If we ponder on those six little words from Genesis 29:30, we will be able to picture the many ways Jacob showed his feelings. But we also see how God communicated His feelings for Leah. As we saw in the last chapter, God stepped in to let Leah know she was valuable to Him by allowing her to bear children. Yet, Leah endured her husband's rejection, so from her we can learn some significant principles for handling rejection:

Face the Facts Realistically

Leah was aware she wasn't loved. She wasn't deceived, and she didn't fool herself. Sometimes we make all kinds of excuses and cover up for the people who rejects us because if we admit their cruelty, it hurts too much. Worse yet, we continue trying to be accepted and as a result face rejection over and over.

Most likely, Leah's longing for Jacob's love probably lasted her entire life, but she learned to live with the situation. Her spiritual voyage led her to reality and acceptance, and her awareness of God indicates a stable relationship growth is reflected in the names she gave her children:

"Leah became pregnant and gave birth to a son. She name him Reuben, for she said, "it is because the Lord has seen my misery. Surely my husband will love me now" (Genesis 29:32). Reuben means, "see a son" but when it is pronounced in Hebrew, it sounds like "He has seen my misery." What does that tell us about Leah's life? She was heartbroken. Pay attention to her heart's cry: "Surely my husband will love me now." We learn something important from her:

Don't Pretend. Confess Your Feelings

To acknowledge the way things are and to admit you would like them to be different are two different situations. It isn't "spiritual" to pretend that everything is fine and you aren't really hurt when you are. Let the Lord know how you feel. He knows it anyway. And, if you are able, share the feelings with

[19]

a reliable person who will pray for you. Both of these trustworthy expressions are important to your emotional and spiritual well being.

In spite of the birth of Reuben, Leah remained unloved. As the story continues, "She conceived again, and when she gave birth to a son she said, "Because the Lord heard that I am not loved, he gave me this one too' So she named him Simeon" (Genesis 29:33).

Simeon means, "One who hears". Leah believed that because the Lord had heard that she was not loved, He had given her another son as a consolation reward. What exactly did God hear? Was Leah told in words that she was unloved? By whom? Did Rachel maliciously remind Leah that she was the booby prize as Rachel's jealousy increased because she was infertile? Or did this mean that Leah told God in her prayers about her rejection? Sadly, both synopsis were probably true.

Before long, Leah had another son: "Again she conceived, and when she gave birth to a son she said, "Now at last my husband will become attached to me because I have borne him three sons." So he was named Levi (Genesis 29:34).

Levi sounds like the word "attached" in Hebrew. This time Leah lowered her expectations. Now she would be fulfilled with just some feeling of genuine connection from Jacob and some appreciation. She never mentions love again. It appears she has finally faced the fact that Jacob would probably never love her as he loved Rachel.

Give Up Unrealistic Expectations

Sometimes we make ourselves sad by visualizing changes that aren't going to take place. Your mother may never be a warm, loving person. Your father may never tell you verbally that he loves you. Your husband may never be able to let down the walls of protection he has built around himself and share the intimacy you desire.

If you spend your life focused on making some other person change, you are wasting your time. The dilemma is not yours; the shortcoming does not lie with you. You are not unworthy. Instead, the other person may be unable and incompetent of the normal responses of an emotionally healthy individual.

We see this happen in Leah when a very important shift occurs in her focus after her fourth son is born: "She conceived again, and when she gave birth to a son she said, "This time I will praise the Lord! So she named him Judah. Then she stopped having children" (Genesis 29:35).

Judah means "praise." After years of suffering, Leah's entire focus turned to God. This time she did not mention Jacob at all; Instead, she got her gut feeling of worth from God. She perceived God valued her because He had proved it to her in a way that was understood in that culture. He granted her children. She was devalued by her father. She was rejected by her husband. She was envied by her sister. But, she was loved by God, and that fact empowered her to go on.

Turn your Focus to God's Acceptance of You

Take a few seconds, open your Bible, and read Ephesians 1:13-14. Notice how special we are to God! We are: Blessed,

[21]

Chosen, Loved, Predestined, Adopted, Redeemed, Forgiven, Lavished with grace, included in Christ, Sealed with the Spirit and Guaranteed an inheritance.

When we put our trust in Christ and form a relationship with Him, He receives us with arms wide open. His acceptance is what gives us worth. It is from Him that we should obtain our self-image.

Do not give a person or persons who reject you authorization to put a price tag on you. God has put His price tag on you. You are worth so much to Him that He chose to come Himself to die for you so you could be His son or daughter, born into His family by faith in Jesus Christ. Follow Leah's model:

Give Thanks to the Lord!

Shortly after that, Leah stopped having children, and she emanated Rachel's lead by giving her maid to Jacob so she could have more sons. Even the names Leah chose for those sons born to her maid revealed a thankful attitude: "Good fortune" and "Happy."

Be Grateful for God's Gifts

Centering on God does not mean we will not ever feel resentment at unfair treatment. Leah was not perfect either. When Rachel attempted to prevent her from having more children by keeping Jacob from sleeping with her, she humiliated herself by "hiring" him for the night with her son's mandrakes. But she also must have prayed, because we read, "God listened to Leah, and she became pregnant and bore Jacob a fifth son. Then Leah said, 'God has rewarded me for

[22]

giving my maidservants to my husband' so she named him Issachar" (Genesis 30:17-18).

I don't think God granted Leah another son because she gave her maid to Jacob. I suspect He answered her prayer mainly because He loved her. Even today, we often have wrong ideas about God, although we have the complete revelation of Scripture. In addition remember, Leah had no Bible. Everything Leah learned about God had been communicated orally, mostly from Jacob, and Jacob obviously didn't understand the grace of God.

And even then God wasn't through showering Leah with His favor: Then Leah said, 'God has presented me with a precious gift. This time my husband will treat me with honor, because I have borne him six sons' So she named him Zebulun." (Genesis 30:20-21).

Another son, and she received him as a precious gift from God. Now she was willing to settle for even less - she just wanted her husband to give her the respect due her as the mother of his six sons. As a special blessing, we read that she also gave birth to a daughter, and she named her Dinah.

How easy it is to ignore God's blessings because there is something we don't have. Sometimes our "if only" blind us to the wonderful provisions we have received, and we refuse to be sincerely grateful.

Life Can Be Unfair

We will all encounter pain in this world if we live long enough. This is a fallen world, and we are a fallen race. There is no way to escape pain and misery. Instead, if we accept it and trust God to use it, He will work it out for our good. God has a way of making restitution for our hurts. And as we learn to handle adversity, our personal character develops.

Leah was the mother of half of Jacob's sons, and half of the twelve tribes of Israel descended from her. Yet, she lived with rejection her entire life - her father's, her husband's, and her sister's. But God confirmed His acceptance of her in a language she could understand by granting her six sons and a daughter.

Jacob chose Rachel, But God chose Leah

Rachel had what Leah yearned for, but it didn't make her a better person. We see no proof of satisfaction or thankfulness in Rachel's life. And there is no reason to presume that she had a relationship with the Lord similar to Leah's. Obviously, the pain of rejection caused Leah to turn to the Lord, and in doing so, she discovered her contentment in Him.

In the end, God had the greatest blessing of all in store for Leah, although she didn't live to see it. God selected Judah, Leah's son, to be the father of the royal dynasty through which His Messiah would be born: Christ, the Son of David, Lion of the tribe of Judah. And, similar to His grandmother generations before Him, Jesus was rejected too.

Chapter Two:
Jesus Experienced
Total Rejection

"He was despised and rejected by men, a man of sorrows, and familiar with suffering... And we esteemed him not" (Isaiah 53:3).

Jesus was perfect in every way. There was no sin, no personality or character flaw in Him that caused Him to be rejected. Yet, He experienced undeserved rejection all His life. Jesus was rejected by His equals, by His half brothers, by His race, by the Gentiles, by the world He had created. In the hour of His torture , He was betrayed by one friend, denied by another, and deserted by all of His disciples. He suffered loneliness, pain, grief, and rejection. "Surely he took up our infirmities and carried our sorrows, yet we considered him stricken by God, smitten by him and afflicted" (Isaiah 53:4).

Why did Jesus lived through such agony? He bore our sins on the cross and took our punishment so that we might be forgiven. But in so doing He encountered the rejection we will never know. He even experienced rejection by God, His

Father. Keep in mind His cry from the cross. "My God! My God! Why have you forsaken me? (Matthew 27:46).

When Jesus became a man, He bore the full punishment for our sin, which is separation from God: "By his wounds we are healed" (Isaiah 53:5).

In the New Testament, we discover more about Jesus' rejection: "Even in his own land and among his own people, he was not accepted. But to all who believed him and accepted him, he gave the right to become children of God" (John 1:11-12).

When you trust Christ as your Savior, you are born into God's family. God accepts you as His beloved child. He loves you with a love that will never fluctuate, falter, or cease. And as you grow in your new life, your great High Priest Jesus intercedes for you with God. Here's the kind of priest He is: "For we do not have a high priest who is unable to sympathize with our weaknesses, but we have one who has been tempted in every way, just as we are - yet without sin. Let us then approach the throne of grace with confidence, so that we may receive mercy and find grace to help us in our time of need" (Hebrew 4:15-16).

Jesus is a Compassionate, Sympathetic Intercessor

Jesus knows how rejection makes us feel. He has been there. He will comfort us, give us value, and use our pain to help others. But to appropriate these gifts, we have to make the kinds of decisions Leah did. We have to give up our expectations, and Focus on God, praising and thanking Him for who He is and for the blessings He showers on us. If we do that, rejection will not be a hindrance to our spiritual growth. It will become a catalyst.

Jesus himself expressed pain over rejection. "O Jerusalem, Jerusalem, you who kill the prophets and stone those sent to you, how often I have longed to gather your children together, as a hen gathers her chicks under her wings, but you were not willing!" (Luke 13:34)

The People Whom Jesus Dwelt Among Were Guilty of Ingratitude Toward Him

The Jews were a favored people above all nations. It was a notable mark of divine favor that the Messiah should be born among them. They should have received Him with delight. His signs and evidence of Messiah-ship were obvious enough. He performed many miracles, and spoke as no other man spoke, yet they rejected Him, treating their best friend as though He had been their worst enemy. This was an overbearing act of national ingratitude.

Special cases occurred in Jesus' life involving still greater ingratitude. Among the people of Israel many became partakers of Jesus' healing power. Many eyes were opened, many deaf ears heard sound; many lame men leaped at His bidding, and many that were sick of palsy and all manner of diseases were suddenly restored by His word. Yet, those who were healed did not become His disciples, for the number of His disciples, after He had ascended, was about one hundred and twenty: yet our Lord, according to the Scriptures many hundreds or thousands had been partakers of His divine power, and yet they did not worship Him. What unyielding disbelief! Strange ingratitude this must have been, that a man should owe

[27]

to Christ his eyesight, and yet refuse to see Jesus as his Savior. Yet so it was, many were healed, but few believed.

We know that our Lord fed thousands of hungry people. He multiplied loaves and fishes and fed crowds, so that they did all eat and were filled. For a time, He was very popular with them, and they would have made Him King, for inactive men much desire a monarch who will supply their needs, and relieve them from personal labor. Yet these people had no love for His doctrine, but followed Him simply alone for what they could get from Him. Many of these selfish followers, most likely, gave their voices against Him and shouted "Crucify Him, crucify Him." They ate bread with Him and lifted up their heel against Him. It is strange that men receiving so much at Jesus' hands should still remain unbelievers in Him.

The same treatment was distributed out to the Lord when He taught the people. He taught them untainted truth in the best possible way, and He made little impact on some. They could not fine fault about His sermons that they were dull and unattractive, and devoid of sympathy. His ministry was pleasing, and mesmerized the ear, yet it was ill received.

When His sermon at Nazareth was finished, they attempted to cast Him down the hill had He not escaped. When He taught the Jews in the temple, "they took up stones again to stone Him" (John 10:31). Some of them sought to trap Him in His speech, and others gnashed their teeth in rage against Him. He brought light into the darkness, and the darkness comprehended it not.

Sometimes, when He found a more select audience than usual, the Lord would preach more deeply into the mysteries, but He

[28]

received no thanks doing this. On one occasion He spoke to them concerning eating His flesh and drinking His blood, but, they turned again to attack Him, and many of those who had followed Him up to that point forsook Him, and walked no longer with Him. Even some disciples who were committed to Him did not always appreciate His sayings. Men returned to Him evil for good, and for the heaped up measure of His kindness, they filled up equally high measure of their hate. For example, when He had healed ten lepers, and only one of them returned to thank Him, -- "Were there not ten cleansed, but where are the nine?" (Luke 17:17). It was the least they could do in return for such matchless deliverance from a deadly disease.

From that unthankful generation the meek and lowly Jesus received no return of love for His temporal and spiritual gifts. Here and there a grateful woman ministered to Him using her resources, and now and then a thankful soul became His disciple; but for the most part, there was no reaction to His love.

Jesus lived to serve man; in obedience to His Father He spent His whole life for men. First, He lived for God's glory, and next for love of men. He forgot Himself, He gave up all ambitious purposes, and gave Himself away so that He might save the lost; and yet, continually, in every way, men sought to take away His life.

At last that evil generation had its way with our Lord Jesus and they took Him after He had been tortured, and led Him away to be crucified. It was the greatest sacrifice that man had ever done for man, and yet the cruel crowd stood around Him, and laughed at His pains, they made jokes about Him, they insulted His faith, they mocked His prayers.

When Jesus died and laid in the grave three days, and had risen again, His rising was for mankind. He could have gone into His glory if He had wanted, but He waited for forty days to minister blessings to His people.

The reaction which He received from the Jewish people was of the same evil character. They questioned whether He had risen from the dead at all, and there were those who made up that idle tale concerning the stealing of His body at night by His disciples. They placed impostors to the door of the Son of God, and charged Jesus with acting a lie.

The case of Judas was especially troubling to Jesus' impressionable soul. In him betrayal reached its climax and despicable ingratitude out did itself. Yet Judas was an apostle, the keeper of His Master's purse, the friend who ate bread with Him and lifted up his heel against Him. "Judas, the one who would betray him, also asked, 'Teacher, I'm not the one, am I?" (Matthew 26:25)

But where were the rest of the disciples, "All the disciples forsook Him and fled" (Matthew 25:56) Peter saw His Master's ill treatment, but he denied Him three times, and added oaths and curses, saying, "I know not the man" (Matthew 26:74). It was like a slap in the face by those whom Jesus had carried for three years and loved even to the end. Those to whom He had opened up His innermost soul, who had eaten with Him His last formal meal before His passion, sought every disciple his own safety, and left Jesus to His fate. The charge lies against all with whom He came in contact, from the worst even to the best.

Fulfilling God's Plan of Jesus

There are too clear and very distinct meanings for the term "will of God" in the Bible. Let us examine some passages of Scripture that make us think this way. First note passages that describe "the will of God" as his sovereign control of all that comes to pass. For example, the way Jesus spoke of the will of God in Gethsemane when he was praying. He said, "My Father, if it be possible, let this cup pass from me, nevertheless, not as I will, but as you will" (Matthew 26:39). What does the will of God refer to in this verse? It refers to the sovereign plan of God that will come to pass in the coming hours. Notice how Acts 4:27-28 says, "Truly in this city they were gathered together against your holy servant Jesus, whom you anointed, both Herod and Pontius Pilate, along with the Gentiles and the peoples of Israel, to do whatever your hand and your plan had predestined to take place." Obviously, the "will of God" was that Jesus die. This was God's plan and His decree. There was no changing it, and Jesus bowed and said, "Yet I want your will, not mine." That's the sovereign will of God.

In addition, it includes the sins of man. Herod, Pilate, the soldiers, the Jewish leaders - they sinned in fulfilling God's will that Jesus be crucified (Isaiah 53:10). God allows to come to pass some things that he hates.

Another example from 1 Peter. Peter writes, "It is better to suffer for doing good, if that should be God's will, than for doing evil" (1 Peter 3:17). In other word, it may be the will of God that Christians suffer for doing good. He sees it as persecution. But persecution of Christians who are persecuted unfairly, is sin. So again, God sometimes allows events to come about that include sin. "It is better to suffer for doing good, if that should be God's will."

Paul gives a brief statement of this truth. He states, "In him (Christ) we have obtained an inheritance, having been predestined according to the purpose of him who works all things according to the counsel of his will" (Ephesians 1:11). The will of God is God's sovereign control of all that come to pass. God's providence over the universe spreads to the smallest details of nature and human choices. Not one sparrow falls to the ground apart from the will of our father in heaven (Matthew 10:29). "The lot is cast into the lap, but its every decision is from the Lord' (Proverbs 16:33). "The plans of the heart belong to man, but the answer of the tongue is from the Lord" (Proverbs 16:1)." "The king's heart is a stream of water in the hand of the Lord; he turns it wherever he will" (Proverbs 21:1).

That's the first meaning of the will of God: it is God's sovereign control of all things. This is called his "sovereign will" or his "will of decree." It cannot be broken. It always come o pass. "He does according to his will among the host of heaven and among the inhabitants of the earth, and none can stay his hand or say to him 'What have you done?" (Daniel 4:35).

Chapter Three:
When The
Unthinkable Happens

There is no doubt that life at times can become devastating; a death of a loved one, loss of a relationship, a pet, job, career, stress, depression, anxiety, diagnosis of a chronic illness or disease, distressing weather conditions, terrifying tragedies or any other unforeseen catastrophe or possible worst case scenario. This can immediately bring on intense stress, disappointment, despair, anxiety, depression and sickness. Denial is not healthy. You must definitely face whatever has happened. It is healthy to mourn or grieve the apparent loss or setback. Momentarily it's okay; but do not stay there. It is not easy when the unthinkable happens. You must first begin to acknowledge what it is you are feeling in order to move forward and embark on to embracing your inner emotional healing.

Yes at some point in time you will experience some type of traumatic experience. But this doesn't have to become the subject of your life. If you are centered you do not have to go into a counter- productive approach. For a season your hands may be tied, rendering a sense of helplessness. You do not want to make life changing decisions while under distress. This will only further complicate your situation and take you further away from resolution. Prepare for change; life is a never ending transition.

It may even get worse before it gets better. But, know it is only a season, at some point it will get better. Therefore when the unthinkable happens you must make a conscious goal to go through it. Not to camp in it. In order to do this you must learn how to depend on someone who is dependable. Although well meaning if you know someone buckles under distress or flies off the handle all the time, they may not be a workable source to help you through. Preferably you need someone who can be objective and knows how to go through a crisis.

God is completely dependable. He is a God of order. He can bring you through crisis and out of it. The one constant you can count on is God. Transitions help us become who we were meant to be. You might ask, where was God when this crisis happened? He is just a prayer away. He is in the same place He was when He allowed His Son to be crucified and die on the cross for the sins of the world. Although He died, He arose with All power. It is because of Jesus we can always have HOPE when going through any crisis.

Planning in advance is great. But I know for a fact no matter how much you plan you cannot avoid the unthinkable. There always something waiting in the shadows. Have you ever heard the saying; "You are either in a storm, coming out of a storm or headed into one..." You do not have to live your

[34]

life in a paranoid state. Life is full of the unexpected. Some by design and some by course. God has given us so many natural ways in which to see His beauty all around us: Look around and begin to enjoy the overabundance of wonderful landscapes about you. They are reminders that life is so much bigger than you and I! God is able. Learn how to persevere, hold on during a traumatic experience and turn to God. Learn how to invite God into your wilderness. This is the time to develop your spiritual muscles.

This is because of God's unfailing love for us that we can count on Him and look to Him when the unthinkable happens. He can turn it around for us. All His promises are true. God has promised to take us through everything. This is the reason it is so important to develop an ongoing relationship with Him. Knowing of God is not the same as knowing God personally. Begin by building an intimate relationship while things are going well. This is the time to develop your healthy managing skills. It is important to learn how to become flexible. We can never totally prepare but we know that life and death are everyday occurrences for someone. This also helps us develop compassion.

Balance is key. However, in order to balance it out we must look on the bright side. You are still here! And there is more to come. As long as there is breath in our bodies we are living beings. The breath of life is a wonderful gift from God. Notice what's around us. God has given us the Seasons to show us how things can change on a regular basis. Just think, it is so pretty after a long cold Winter. A beautiful fresh Spring comes forth bringing new life with it. Then a long hot Summer comes welcoming a nice cool Fall. "In this greatly rejoice, though now for a little while, if we need be, you have been

[35]

grieved with various tests, that the genuineness of your Faith, being more precious than gold that perishes, though it is tested by fire, may be found to praise , honor, and glory at the revelation of Jesus Christ, whom having not seen you love. Though you do not see Him, yet believing, you rejoice with joy inexpressible and full of glory, receiving the end of your Faith; the Salvation of your souls." *Once we realize that we were meant to live life to please God it really makes all the difference in the world. When the unthinkable happens, you really can make it! Remember, there is more in store. You can always count on His Word. God's love lasts through eternity: When we have God on our side, we have everything we will ever need. Absolutely nothing gets by Him that comes our way. Everything is under His control and His promise to never leave or forsake us is so true. 1Peter 1 says:*

"All flesh is as grass, And all glory of man as the flower of the grass, The grass withers, And its flowers falls away, But the Word of the Lord endures forever."

When Our World Falls Apart

Ironically, even though we know that life happens, we rarely expect life to happen to us in the way it often does. Traumatic situations can shake us to the very core of our being. They can interfere with our sense of what's real to come crashing down and they can replace our zeal for life with an overwhelming, overpowering burden that leaves us feeling numb.

One thing you can count on is that life will happen. It will introduce any number of situations that bring in pain and feelings of hopelessness. The question is how will you

[36]

respond? Will you become bitter or better? Will your faith in God flunk the test or pass with flying colors? Will you melt in the fire like plastic or become strong and refined like steel? These are some questions life will force you to answer.

The Bible states that we will face tribulation in this life (Acts 14:22). Tribulation does not play favorites based on ethnicity, gender, or socioeconomic status. The professional, pastor, politician, business owner, blue-collar worker, athlete, and soccer mom care equally weak to economic devastation, divorce, incurable disease, betrayal, infidelity, demonic attacks. God is the same yesterday, today and forever. There is nothing too hard for God. Whether you are facing financial chaos, infidelity, a bad medical report, or the death of a loved one, God is still on the throne to heal and renew you with living water in the midst of your storm. God is able to influence life.

The stone the builders rejected became your chief cornerstone (Psalm 118:22; Mark 12:10). In your rejected state you learned to depend on God. Yet God became your daily bread. He remained close and remained real when nothing else was making sense. Because of His hand on your life you matured enough to see that your hope was never supposed to be in your husband, friends, or church members but in God alone. When you truly understood this, you learned to love and forgive those who betrayed and hurt you.

God is at work in our lives even when we can't see Him. He knows the ending of everyone's story before the beginning. We have learned to trust what we can see and feel, but God wants us to trust Him and His word.

Never doubt the presence and activity of God in our lives. God has more supernatural warriors fighting for us than Satan has fighting against us. He allows these seasons to strengthen us as we learn to depend on Him. You must know your life is in the hands of our everlasting Father. Trust Him to take care of you in your valley experience, and be obedient to His voice.

You learned that your life was never attached to a person; your life, destiny, and purpose were always wrapped in God. As a result, you are not a slave to man's opinion of yourself.

Forgiveness doesn't exonerate the one who hurt you nor does it trivialize the depth of your trauma. Not at all. What it does do is liberate you and your soul from living in the Haunted House of memories and agonies that aren't worthy of more lost time in your life. Forgiveness is a gift you must find a way to give yourself regardless of who or what has drove you into this grievous state of affairs.

So, then forgiveness is important if we are to grow into the fullness of who God created us to be. As we are made in his image, we share his capacity to love, to experience, betrayal from those we love, and to extend forgiveness and risk loving again. Forgiveness isn't about weakening you but strengthening you to live again, performing at your highest potential, unencumbered by yesterday's maladies. I want to guide you back to your fullest capacity and stop the brain drain and agony of a wild memory. And help you regain your control as you do have enormous power to change the quality and direction of your own life, away from the path of soul deterioration and bitterness and toward the spiritual healing of grace and peacefulness.

Chapter Four:
Having The Mind
of Christ

One of the instructions given to us in the Bible is to have the mind of Christ. The Bible states, "Let this mind be in you which was also in Christ Jesus" (Philippians 2:5). Have you ever pondered how this is obtainable? Surely, we know how important it is. God created the human mind as a combination of conscious and unconscious thoughts of the brain that guide our mental and physical behavior. Our thoughts influence our actions. So the bottom line then, that if we want to act like Christ, we must also think like Him.

With the mind we employ the power of reason, conceive ideas and exercise judgment. It stows our intellect, as distinguished from the emotion or will.

There are many rewards to having the mind of Christ, "in whom are hidden all the treasures of wisdom and knowledge" (Colossian 2:3). Here are a few others:

Romans 8:6 tells us that "to be spiritually minded is life and peace."
Isaiah 1:18 says that God wants us to come and reason with Him. He wants us to know His will for our lives.
Psalms 119:33-37, The psalmist asked God to give him understanding in keeping His laws and walking in His commandments so that he might "turn away... from looking at worthless things." Having any mind other

[39]

than Christ's causes us to live a life of disobedience and rebellion.

David Wilkerson defines: "Rebellion... is a refusal to seek God's mind in all things. We can never obtain the mind of God by relying on our own reasoning."

To have the mind of Christ, we must think as He thinks. This is difficult for us because our thoughts are not God's thoughts (Isaiah 55:8). The support for our beliefs, ideas and paradigms are based on perceptions of reality that were developed in our families of origin and life experiences.

If the people and circumstances that influenced our mental thinking were godly, we will find it easier to fix our thoughts on Jesus. On the other hand, if we were raised under dysfunctional, abusive conditions, we may struggle with evil, carnal thoughts. This is certain death to living a godly life, as the Bible states, "to be carnally minded is death" (Romans 8:6).

Having the mind of Christ shows any distorted thinking we may have. Otherwise we are subject to our carnal minds. And the carnal mind can't understand the spiritual mind (Romans 8;6-7).

Renewing the Mind

The Bible tells us how it is possible to have the mind of Christ in spite of our life history. We are to "be transform by the renewing of our minds" (Romans 12:2).

One way we can use to renew our minds is to meditate on God's Word. Psalms 199:20, 24 states, "My soul is consumed with longing for your laws at all times. Your statues are my delight; they are my counselors." Like the psalmist, we can find joy and knowledge in the Word when we choose to dwell on it.

One of the most important methods we can renew our minds is to think on the things that are mentioned in Philippians 4:8: "Whatever is true, whatever is noble, whatever is right, whatever is pure, whatever is lovely, whatever is admirable - if anything is praiseworthy - think about such things.

God is a God of truth. In fact, the Bible states it is impossible for Him to lie (Hebrew 6:18). He gives us His truth in every situation to apply to our thoughts. "And you shall know the truth, and the truth shall make you free" (John 8:32). If you are not free, ask yourself which lie of the devil are you believing as truth in your life?

Remember, we live our lives according to our perception of what is true - according to what we perceive is real. But if our perceptions are false, if we do not think on the truths of God, we will easily be led astray by Satan's deceptions and counterfeits.

Philippians 4:7 says that the peace of God guards our minds. I believe that one reason God protects us in this way is that wrong thoughts are a breeding ground for Satan's lies. Another name for Satan is deceiver. He can imitate truth, but "there is no truth in him" (John 8:44).

We are not exempt to "the devil's schemes" (Ephesians 6:11). In fact, we must constantly be on guard lest "just as Eve was deceived by the serpent's cunning, our minds may somehow be led astray"   (2 Corinthians 11:3). Thank God for the Holy Spirit. It is the Holy Spirit who reveals the lies of the enemy that we hear and receive as truth.

[41]

Thoughts vs. Feelings

How can you know if what you are hearing is the truth or a lie? One method is to determine the difference between what you think and what you feel.

Paul says that Christ will dwell in our hearts and that we will know the love of Christ so that we may be filled with all the fullness of God. Both feeling and thinking are important.

One way we can use to help us separate our thoughts from our emotions is validation. When we validate ourselves, we are acknowledging our feelings. You say, "I feel" and then finish the statement with a word that expresses feelings such as "lonely," "angry," or "sad."

Feelings are necessary. They are given by God in order for us to experience emotions. The Bible reveal to us that Jesus experienced joy, wept and had righteous anger. But He distinguished His emotions from reason, and so must we.

Let's examine the feeling of anger. Anger was created as an internal alarm to warn us of potentially threatening situations.

To feel anger is not a sin (Ephesians 4:26). But the ungodly behavior that often accompanies the emotion of anger is sin. For example, if we discipline our children by using our anger in ways that devalue them, discourage them or provoke them to anger, we misuse the emotion.

The feeling of fear is another internal alarm. But if we allow feelings of fear to paralyze us from taking biblical action, such as confronting someone in truth and love about their abusive behavior toward us, we misuse the emotion.

[42]

Although feelings are important, we should not allow them to control our behavior!

Many Christians respond as the world responds. Usually, the world's procedure for living is "if it feels good, do it." Their thought process looks like this: My thoughts... my feelings... my actions.

But the method of a Christian who has the mind of Christ is "I know what I think and how I feel, but I will do what God says to do." That process looks like this: My thoughts... my feelings... God's thoughts... my actions.

The second set of thoughts is based on God's Word (Hebrew 4:12) - aligning our thoughts with His thoughts before we act. "A prudent man gives thought to his steps" (Proverbs 14:15).

Discerning the Truth

Let me give an example of how this work in real life. A husband and wife exchange harsh words. The wife says, "I feel you don't love me." In actuality, the idea that her husband doesn't love her is a thought, not a feeling. The feeling is most likely hurt or rejection.

The wife needs to examine her belief from a rational perspective. Is the thought that her husband doesn't love her the truth or a lie? Usually it is a lie of the enemy to put spouses at odds with one another.

The truth of the matter is that her husband does love her but needs to learn ways to demonstrate to his wife his love in order to reduce her feelings of hurt and rejection. If the wife is able to see this truth, she can cast down an argument that goes "against the knowledge of God, bringing every thought into

[43]

captivity to the obedience of Christ" (2 Corinthian 10:5). What could have escalated into a war can become fruitful ground for oneness, growth and change.

Learning to substitute the lies of Satan with God's truth is key to having the mind of Christ and living a life that is pleasing to God. God will honor you as you seek to line up your thoughts with His. "I the Lord search the heart and examine the mind, to reward a man according to his conduct, according to what his deeds deserve" (Jeremiah 17:10).

Ask the Lord, with the help of the Holy Spirit, to show you the lies you have been believing and living out in your life. Replace the lies with God's truths so that your relationship with Him, yourself and others will become better enhanced.

The Mind of Christ vs. the Mind of Satan

Our mindset determines how we live and what our values are. God's mindset is love toward His creation. Love is an outward focus and the way of giving. Satan is selfish. Selfishness is an inward focus and the way of getting. Paul instructed the Philippians to put away selfishness. To not do anything through selfish goals or conceit. To look out for the interests of others. To esteem others better than ourselves. He described that as taking on the mind of Christ (Philippians 2:1-11).

We can take the difference between the mind of Satan and the mind of Christ another step further by considering Proverbs 29:11 "A fool vents all his feelings, but a wise man holds them back." Christ's way of loving and giving includes exercising restraint. Satan's way of selfishness and getting is to cast off restraint. Esau is described as a irreverent and disrespectful

[44]

person who sold his birthright for one morsel of food. He traded his magnificent future promise for just a moment's satisfaction. Later, when he wanted to inherit the blessing, there was no going back. His desire for immediate gratification caused him very deep regrets (Hebrews 12:14-17).

Works of the Flesh vs. Fruit of the Spirit

Our flesh screams out to be satisfied but, in responding, we must be careful to act with restraint. The works of the flesh include outbursts of wrath and selfish ambition, while the fruit of the spirit includes exercising self-control (Galatians 5:19-24). The works of the flesh and the fruit of the spirit take us in totally different directions.

Exodus 32 is the account of Israel worshipping before the golden calf that Aaron made. The account reveals that after Aaron constructed the molded calf and declared a feast, the people sat down to drink and rose up to play. It says that Aaron had not restrained them. As a result, God determined to destroy them, but Moses begged on their behalf. Verse 14 records, "So the Lord relented from the harm which He said He would do to His people." God punished Israel for their sin, but even in correction, He exercised restraint. He continued to work with them as His people. It is instructive that God sent a plague on Israel when they gave themselves up to craving for meat (Numbers 11), but He was going to destroy them for idolatry. There is a difference between temporarily giving in to sin and making provision to sin day after day. Still, as difficult as any battle may be, we must not make provision for sin. Paul listed doing so as being in opposition to putting on the mind of Christ (Romans 13:11-14).

[45]

Eli was a priest and a judge in Israel when the tabernacle stood in Shiloh. His sons were disrespectful and corrupt and they troubled the people when they came to make sacrifices and to give offerings. They even had sex with some of the women. It ultimately cost them their lives. It cost Eli dearly as well. By giving in to them in their sin he brought a curse of suffering and death on his descendants, and his lineage was removed from the priesthood. Even though Eli had warned his sons against what they were doing, he took no action. The Bible says, "His sons made themselves vile, and he did not restrain them" (1 Samuel 3:13). It is not enough for us to just refuse to do evil. We must also choose to do good.

The importance of our mindset can hardly be ignored. The words we say, the example we set and the actions we take impact our future and the future of those around us.

In this life we can strive to give, or we can seek to get. We can be outwardly focused, or we can be self-focused. We can exercise restraint in the fear of God, or we can cast off restraint. These choices all have one thing in common. They portray the difference between the mind of Satan and the mind of Jesus Christ.

Chapter Five:
The Favor of God

Favor is a grace you must purposely ask God for. Many people are talented, but many are also without favor. Talent, skill or knowledge cannot take the place of favor. They are good and can take us far. However, the favor of God surpasses them all. On the other hand, in addition to your skill, talent and hard work will take you to greater heights. The head of the household in the Bible always prayed for favor in the eyes of God and men. They were aware of it. They understood the covenant of favor and its effect in their lives. Mary became the channel through which Jesus entered the world because was highly favored by God. Esther also was favored by God and man. Once you are favored by God, you will receive the best job on the earth. But if you are favored by men, you will be given the best task.

Favor does not mean laziness or receiving blessings without working. It simply means you will be allowed to use your talents and gifts. "See thou a man diligent in his business? He shall stand before kings; he shall not stand before mean men" (Proverbs 22:29). Favor takes any hardworking person to greater heights. You may be gifted or skilled, yet you will need favor to reach the height of whatever you do.

The Bible states, "I returned and saw under the sun that the race is not to the swift, nor the battle to the strong, neither yet to the wise, nor yet riches to men of understanding, nor yet favor to men of skill, but time and chance happen to them all." (Ecclesiastes 9:11). Bread, riches and favor come from God directly. It is God who rewards our hard work. Declare the favor of God in all you do relentlessly. When you are favored, people will want to associate with you. And when you are favored, people will not deal hard with you even when you make mistakes. Many people have been fired from their jobs because they did not have divine favor. Favor is a shield that protects and surrounds every area of your life. It is like assets that allow you to move on even when mistakes have been made. It is a must have. Favor hands you the big assignment. It lends to you all you need in life. Favor guarantees that people do not go out empty handed out of a place where they have worked. People get hurt when they are not rewarded. The hurt and bitterness show them a lot of negative energy and influence.

Favor is not bias. It is just favor. Whatever it is God has blessed you with, it is protected by His mercy and favor. Favor is referred to us as grace in some parts of the Bible. "Let us therefore come boldly unto the throne of grace, that we may obtain mercy and find grace to help in time of need." (Hebrews 4:16). Every need in your life will be met when God's favor is reveal on you. After receiving favor, you must also work. This reveals that you truly earn to have what you received. For example, you must do the job in the best possible way. Favor brings a good name. Put relationships above money. The more you get money, the more lasting relationships you should build. The richest man is the one with powerful relationships.

The Bible states, "And God is able to make all grace abound toward you; that ye, always having all sufficiency in all things may abound to every good work: (As it is written, He

[48]

hath dispersed abroad; he hath given to the poor: his righteousness remains forever." (2 Corinthians 9:8-90). Finally, we must note that we also receive favor when we give. Grace in the above means favor. When you give, ask God to reward you with favor in the eyes of men that you may abound in every good work. Then, you will experience abundance. Pray always for the favor of God over your life and you will fully enjoy the blessings of God.

The Favor of God will Produce Blessings

We through life endeavor to receive the favor of people whether we are trying to get an account or a young man interested in a young lady, a child with his father, a student with his teacher, worker with his boss, etc. However, we should mostly strive to get favor of God by doing His will. The following is 10 blessings that come with God's favor:

> God's favor can produce Supernatural increase and promotion.
> **Genesis 39:21** says, "But the Lord was with Joseph and showed him mercy, and gave him favor in the sight of the keeper of the prison.
> It brings Restoration of everything the enemy has stolen.
> **Exodus 3:21** says, "And I will give this people favor in the sight of the Egyptians, and it shall come to pass that when ye go, ye shall not go empty.
> **Psalms 105:37** says, "He brought them forth also with silver and gold, and there was not one feeble person among their tribes.

John 10:10 says "The thief cometh not but for to steal, and to kill, and to destroy: I am come that they might have life, and that they might have it more abundantly.

It brings Honor in the midst of adversaries.

Exodus 11:3 says, "And the Lord gave the people favor in the sight of the Egyptians. Moreover, the man Moses was very great in the land of Egypt in the sight of Pharaoh's servants, and in the sight of the people.

It can produce increased assets.

Deuteronomy 33:23 says, "And of Naphtali, he said, O Naphatali, satisfied with favor, and full with the blessing of the Lord: possess thou the west and the south.

It can give great and unusual victories even against impossible odds.

Joshua 6:20 says, "So the people shouted when the priests blew with the trumpets, and it came to pass, when the people heard the sound of the trumpet, and the people shouted with a great shout, that the wall fell down flat, so the people went up into the city, every man straight before him, and they took the city.

Joshua 10:9 says, "Joshua therefore came unto them suddenly, and went up from Gilgal all night. And the Lord discomforted them before Israel, and slew them with a great slaughter at Gibeon, and chased them along the way that goes up to Beth Horon, and smote them to Azekah, and unto Makkedah.

6. God's favor can give recognition and promotion even when you seem to be the least likely one to receive it.

1 Samuel 16:22 says, "And Saul sent to Jesse saying, Let David I pray thee, stand before me; for he hath found favor in my sight.

7.　　It can produce prominence and preferential treatment, favor and kindness.

Esther 5:8 says, "If I have found favor in the sight of the king, and if I please the king to grant my petition, and to perform my request, let the king and Haman come to the banquet that I shall prepare for them, and I will do tomorrow as the king hath said.

8.　　Get petitions granted , even by ungodly civil authority.
(See the above scripture).
9.　　It can change rules, regulations, even laws if necessary to your advantage.

Esther 8:5 says, "And said if it please the king, and if I have found favor in his sight, and the

thing seem right before the king, and I be pleasing in his eyes, let it be written to reverse

the letters devised by Haman the son of Hammedatha the Agagite, which he wrote to

destroy the Jews which are in all the king's provinces.
10. His favor can win battles you did not even have to fight because God will fight them for you.

Psalms 44:1-3 (Read it).
It is not wrong when we seek the favor of men, however, it is most rewarding when we strive for the favor of God in our lives. How?
- Study the Word of God.

[51]

- Be a doer of the Word.
- Pray daily and be filled continually with His Holy Spirit.
- Then, you can be led by the Spirit.
- Tell others what Christ means to you.

This is a good start in bringing the favor of God in your life. Remember Enoch, before God translated him, he had a testimony that pleased God.

Chapter Six: The Authority of the Believer

God has given the believer authority and victory in both the natural and spiritual realm. Observe what it says in the following verses, (Ephesians 1:19) "And his incomparably great power for us who believe. That power is like the working of his mighty strength, (20) which he exerted in Christ when he raised him from the dead and seated him at his right hand in the heavenly realms, (21) far above all rule and authority, power and dominion, and every title that can be given, not only in the present age but also in the one to come. (22) And God placed all things under his feet and appointed him to be head over everything for the church, (23) which is his body, the fullness of him who fills everything in every way." (2:6) "And God raised us up with Christ and seated us with him in the heavenly realms in Christ Jesus."

I dare you to read, meditate on and memorize the above scriptures constantly. These verses will increase your faith, and encourage you because of who you are and what you have in Christ. (See also Hebrews 2:5-8; Luke 10:17-19; Ephesians 4:27; Joshua 1:3; 2 Corinthians 10:4-5; Revelation 12:11; 1 John 4:4/5:4-5; Romans 8:37; Deuteronomy 28:7-13).

The devil has been harassing many of us. I love Romans 16:20 which says, "And the God of peace shall soon crush Satan under your feet." Observe it says, God of peace. At times the only way to make peace is to fight. I believe this is a prophetic word to many who are reading this. God is fighting on your behalf, and is about to place Satan and all his demons under your feet.

Areas where you should exercise your authority:

Life and prosperity (John 10:10; Deuteronomy 30:15 & 19; 3 John 2) Jesus came that we might experience life more abundantly than we ever could outside of Him. This has to do with much more than just money. It involves every area of our life - spiritually, mentally, emotionally, physically and materially.

Health and wholeness (Isaiah 53:3-5; Psalms 103:1-5; Romans 8:11) "By His stripes we are healed" (Isaiah 53:5). The frame of reference deals with more than physical healing but emotional and mental as well. Someone who is battling emotional scars God can completely deliver you right now. Perhaps someone else has been told you have a mental illness that God can also heal as you read this. Receive your deliverance now by faith. The same Spirit that raised Jesus from the dead is about to bring life to someone's physical body (Romans 8:11).

Finances (2 Corinthians 9:6-8; Philippians 4:18-19; Deuteronomy 8:11-20). It is He who gives you the power to make wealth" (Deuteronomy 8:18). Wait for Him to speak to you. If you hear something, it may be Him giving you just what you need. Seek advice, pray and if everything seems to be a go, run with it.

God is able to make all financial favor overflow toward you (2 Corinthians 9:8) and open the windows of heaven blessing you until there is no longer room to receive it (Malachi 3:10). He promises to supply all your need according to His riches in glory (Philippians 4:18-19). It should be observed that in each of these verses it deals with giving. We cannot expect God to surround us with favor and meet our needs if we are not willing to first be faithful in our giving.

Salvation of our family and loved ones (Acts 2:38-39; 16:31; Isaiah 59:21).

The enemy has robbed us of our loved ones long enough. Let's stand on the Word of God for them to be brought to Jesus. He can even reach "those that are afar off (Acts 2:39).

Growth of the body of Christ (Isaiah 43:5-7; Acts 2:39; Ephesians 4:16). It is God's desire and will that the church grow both spiritually and numerically. If you will be faithful, pray, witness, follow up on the delinquents, diligent and believe God, He will make the church body to grow. He has ordained that you should go and bring forth fruit and that your fruit should remain" (John 15:16). Notice, you have to go in order to increase. It will not happen with you sitting on the sidelines and doing nothing.

Peace and joy (John 14:27; 16:33; Ephesians 2:14). Go over these scriptures. God's desire you to have peace and joy. All of what is listed here and above may not be manifest in your life at every given moment. God desires to give you peace and joy even when these things aren't a reality in your life. There are times when we have to break forth into joy" (Isaiah 59:9), even when there is nothing to be joyful about.

Implementing Our Authority as Believers

Now that we've discussed the authority we have in Christ, I want to share how we can implement that authority.

Look in the book of Ephesians and count how many times Paul mentions "in Christ," "in Him," and "in Jesus." The entire first half of Ephesians Paul is attempting to help us realize who we are in Christ -before ever revealing to us what we are to do for him.

How to implement the authority given to us in the heavenly realm into the realm of reality (Ephesians 1:19-23; 2:6; Joshua 1:3; Ephesians 4:27). "Thou hast put all things in subjection under his feet. For in that he put all things in subjection under him, he left nothing that is not put under him"(Hebrews 2:8). It is clear in this verse that God has placed all things in subjection to us, under our feet. "But now see not yet all things not under him," also reveals it hasn't completely materialized yet. Therefore, there must be something we can do to bring this into the realm of reality. Below are a number of things to help us start moving in that direction.

Tenacity and discipline (2 Timothy 4:6-8; Galatians 6:9; Luke 18:1). This is not always easy, It is something I have struggled with, especially in recent years. The real struggle is in maintaining your authority. It takes fight, discipline and downright determination. It is hard when we face battles and things don't turn out right, to continue standing firm and implement our authority in the situations of life. It is easy to become discouraged, fainthearted and give up instead of continuing to fight the good fight of faith.

This is especially hard when we face continuous hardships and let downs in our life. It is easy to get weary and worn out. Even when we have been very tenacious in the past, we have a difficult time to get back up and moving forward again. We must reach deep down within ourselves as David did, and encouraged himself in the Lord (1 Samuel 30:6). This was a major turning point for David. If he had failed to do this, he would have missed God and the greatness God had prepared for him. It is in the very beginning of 2 Samuel that David is crowned king. This happened partly because of his tenacity.

Choose life (Deuteronomy 30:19). Life and victory is mainly a choice. Things will not always go right for us. We will be attacked and sometimes viciously. We may get and feel beat down and defeated. We may even get disappointed and depressed. We may feel there is no way out and hopeless.

It is at these times we must choose life. This is the only way to pull out of the trap we are in and begin to head toward and experience victory. Yell it out at the top of your lungs. "I choose life." We must choose life and keep choosing life until we have taken authority over our situation and victory has come.

Visualizing your victory (John 5:17 & 19; Judges 6:11-12; Proverbs 29:18). As with productive praying, we must see the victory in the spiritual realm before it can become an outward reality. Jesus saw the Father working and therefore He worked (John 5:17 & 19). Gideon was hiding in the wine press for fear of the Midianites. When the angel called him he said, "The Lord is with thee thou mighty man of valor" (Judges 6:11-12).

I remember when my principal was doing everything to get me to quit. Every time he would say something negative to me, I use to say, "God was working this out for my good." I believe my principal thought I was crazy since I did not allow his actions to distract me from getting God's best for me.

[57]

Although everything in my life, at the time, was turned upside down, I knew that God allowed Satan to do it.

Exercise faith. If we are to implement the authority given to us in Christ, we must be men and women of faith. It was said of Abraham, "Who against hope believed in hope" (Romans 4:18). "We walk by faith not by sight" (2 Corinthians 5:7). To declare our authority in the affairs of life, our faith must be expressed in four ways:

5 Reasons Believers Don't Walk in Power

Here are five reasons believers don't walk in the power and authority they have in Christ:

1. Sin. When we practice sin, we come under Satan's authority, and he has legal rights over us until we repent. That is why Jesus said, "The ruler of the world is coming, and has nothing on Me" (John 14:30). Jesus was without sin, so the devil could not get a stronghold in His life.

James 5:16 declares, "The effective fervent prayer of a righteous man avails much." This verse points out that authority is given to the righteous.

Along the same line, we must be under authority before we can exercise authority. If we are rebellious toward God, our parents or the authority of our church, we won't have much authority over the evil one.

2. Ignorance. In Hosea 4:6 God declares, "My people are destroyed for lack of knowledge." The Lord showed me that His people are being destroyed by ignorance of their authority in Christ. Yet the Bible is clear that we are not powerless against the enemy.

[58]

2 Corinthians 10:3-5 states, "For though we walk in the flesh, we do not war according to the flesh. For the weapons of our warfare are not carnal but mighty in God for pulling down strongholds, casting down arguments and every high thing that exalts itself against the knowledge of God, bringing every thought into captivity to the obedience of Christ.

Many believers tend to see the never- ending struggle through the lens of the Asian philosophy of yin and yang which contends that good and evil forces are opposite each other but equal in power and authority. In reality, Satan is a loser. He is a created being, one of God's fallen angels.

God on the other hand, is the uncreated Creator who always has been and will be - He is self-existent. To a believer who is walking in God's authority, Satan is like a toothless lion. It is not that Satan doesn't have some real power - he does. But when we compare his power with God's - there is no comparison.

When David confronted Goliath, Goliath compared his physical ability with David's. Goliath was insulted that the Israelites would send a mere shepherd boy against him.

However, David didn't compare himself with Goliath; he compared Goliath with God. God was so much greater than Goliath that the match was over before it had a chance to begin (1 Samuel 17:41-50).

In observing God's people, I have noticed that way to many of us to be ignorant about the source of evil. Satan, not God, is the cause of all the evil in the world. When we have a warp perspective of the sovereignty of God, we become passive in fighting sickness and evil.

[59]

After the evil of 9/11 tragedy, I was amazed to discover how many people blamed the terrorist attacks to God's judgment. The Bible tells us that Satan - not God, is the one who comes to kill, steal and destroy (John 10:10) and that we are to put on the full armor of God and stand firm against the evil one (Ephesians 6:10-18).

3. Unbelief. Unbelief is a serious sin. Romans 14:23 states, "But the man who has doubts is condemned if he eats, because his eating is not from faith, and everything that does not come from faith is sin." The book of Hebrews also calls unbelief sinful: "See to it, brothers, that none of you has a sinful, unbelieving heart that turns away from the living God." (3:12). Unbelief is so serious that Jesus could not do many miracles because the people's lack of faith (Matthew 13:58).

We can measure the level of our belief or unbelief by asking ourselves, Do we really believe that Jesus defeated the enemy? If we don't, we are unlikely to see the results we desire when we lay hands on the sick.

4. Fear. 2 Timothy 1:7-8 declares, "God has not given us a spirit of fear." Fear paralyzes us and keeps us from exercising the authority we have in Christ to bring healing to others.

1 John 5:18 teaches that, "the wicked one does not touch (born-again believers). But some people have suffered backlash from the enemy when they engaged in spiritual warfare and are now afraid.

There are many reasons for backlash. Here are some ways to guard against it: Be led by the Spirit; make sure that Satan has no legal right to attack; and obtain prayer covering.

[60]

After taking these steps, we can confront the darkness because we have the authority to do so. We need not to be afraid of obeying God's directives even if it requires engaging in strategic warfare.

Luke 12:32 gives us wise counsel: "Do not be afraid, little flock, for it is your Father's good pleasure to give you the kingdom.

5. Prayerlessness. Luke 18:1 establishes the importance of prayer. "Then Jesus told His disciples a parable to show them that they should always pray and not give up."

Ephesians 6:18 elaborates on this point: "And pray in the Spirit on all occasions with all kinds of prayers and requests. With this in mind, be alert and always keep on praying for all the saints."

There is a lesson here for all of us. When we know who God is and the authority He has, and when we know who we are in Christ, having faith is not difficult. And when we have faith, we will begin to release the spiritual authority necessary to perform signs, wonders and miracles.

Chapter Seven: The Faithfulness of God

Unfaithfulness is one of the most extraordinary sins of these evil days. In the business world, a man's word is no longer his bond. In the social world, marital infidelity overflows on every hand, the sacred bonds of wedlock being broken with as little regard as the discarding of an old garment. In the ministerial realm, thousands who have solemnly agreed to preach the truth make no second thought to attack and deny it. Neither reader or writer can claim complete immunity from this fearful sin: in how many ways we have been unfaithful to Christ, and to the light and privileges which God has committed to us. How refreshing, then, how unspeakably blessed, to lift our eyes above the scene of ruin, and behold One who is faithful, faithful in all things, faithful at all times. "Know therefore that the Lord thy God, He is God, the faithful God" (Deuteronomy 7:9). This quality is important to His being, without it, He would not be God.

For God to be unfaithful would be to act contrary to His nature which were impossible: "If we believe not, yet, He abides faithful; He cannot deny Himself" (2 Timothy 2:13). Faithfulness is one of the glorious perfections of His being. He

[62]

as it were clothed with it: "O Lord God of hosts, who is a strong Lord like unto Thee? or to Thy faithfulness round about Thee?" (Psalms 89:8). So when God became incarnate it was said, "Righteous shall be the girdle of His loins, and faithfulness the girdle of His reins" (Isaiah 11:5). What a word that is in Psalm 36:5, Thy mercy, "O Lord, is in the heavens; and Thy faithfulness unto the clouds." Far above all finite comprehension is the unchanging faithfulness of God. Everything about God is great, vast, and incomparable. He never forgets, never fails, never falters, never forfeits His word. To every declaration of promise or prophesy the Lord has exactly observed, every engagement of covenant or threatening He will make good, for "God is not a man that He should lie; neither the son of man, that He should repent: hath He said, and shall He not do it? or hath He spoken, and shall He not make it good? (Numbers 23:19). Therefore does the believer exclaim, "His compassions fail not, they are new every morning: great is Thy faithful " (Lamentations 3:22, 23).

Scripture overflows in illustrations of God's faithfulness. More than four thousand years ago He said, "While the earth remains, seedtime and harvest, and cold and heat, and summer and winter, day and night shall not cease" (Genesis 8:22). Every year that comes turns out a fresh witness to God's fulfillment of this promise. In Genesis we see that Jehovah declared to Abraham, "Thy seed shall be a stranger in a land that is not theirs, and shall serve them... But in the fourth generation, they shall come hither again" (vv. 13-16). Centuries ran their weary course. Abraham's descendants moaned among the brick-kilns of Egypt. Had God forgotten His promise? No, see Exodus 12:41, "And it came to pass at the end of the four hundred and thirty years, even the self-same day it came to pass that all the hosts of the Lord went out from the land of Egypt." Through Isaiah the Lord declared, "Behold, a virgin shall conceive, and bear a son , and shall His name Immanuel" (7-14). Again centuries pass, but "When the fullness of time was come, God sent forth His son, made of a woman" (Galatians 4:4). God is true, His Word of Promise is sure. With all His relationships with His people God is faithful. He may be safely relied upon. No one ever yet really trusted Him in vain. We find this precious truth expressed almost everywhere in the Scriptures, for His people need to know that faithfulness is an important part of the Divine character of God. This is the basis of our confidence in Him.

But it is one thing to accept the faithfulness of God as a Divine truth, it is quite another to act on it. God has given us many "exceedingly great and precious promises," but are we really counting on His fulfillment of them? Are we actually expecting Him to do for us all that He has said? Are we resting with implied assurance on these words, "He is faithful that promised" (Hebrew 10:23)? There are seasons in the lives of all when it is not easy, no not even for Christians to believe that God is faithful. Our faith is greatly tried, our eyes dimmed with tears, and we can no longer trace the workings of His love. Our ears are distracted with the noises of the world, harassed by the atheistic whispering of Satan, and we can no longer hear the sweet accents of Jesus' still small voice. Cherished plans have been hindered, friends on whom we relied have failed us, a protest brother or sister in Christ has betrayed us. We are overwhelmed. We sought to be faithful to God, and now a dark cloud hides Him from us. We find it difficult, yes, even impossible, for carnal reason to unify His providence with His gracious promises. A faltering soul, severely-tried fellow pilgrim, seek grace to heed Isaiah 50:10, "Who is among you that fears the Lord, that obeys the voice of His servant, that walks in darkness and has no light? let him trust in the name of the Lord, and rely upon his God."

When you are tempted to doubt the faithfulness of God, cry out, "Get thee behind me, Satan." Though you cannot now unify God's mysterious dealings with the declaration of His love, wait on Him for more light. In His own good time He will make it plain to you. "What I do thou know not now, but thou shall know here after" (John 13:7). The follow-up will yet demonstrate that God has neither forsaken nor deceived His child. "And therefore will the Lord wait that He may be gracious to you, and therefore will He be exalted, that He may have mercy upon you: for the Lord is a God of judgment: blessed are all they that wait for Him" (Isaiah 30:18). "Thy testimonies which Thou has commanded are righteous and very faithful" (Psalm 119:138). God has not only told us the best, but He has not withheld the worst. He has faithfully described the ruin which the fall has affected. He has faithfully diagnosed the terrible state which sin has produced. He has faithfully made known His long-standing hatred of evil, and that He must punish the same. He has faithfully warned us that He is a consuming fire" (Hebrew 12:29). Not only does His word overflow in illustrations of His fidelity in fulfilling His promises, but it also records numerous examples of His faithfulness in making good His scary warnings. Every stage of Israel's history demonstrates that solemn fact. So it was with individuals: Pharaoh, Korah, Achon, and a hosts of others are so many proofs. And thus it will be with you, my reader: unless you have fled or do flee to Christ for refuge, the everlasting burning of the Lake of Fire will be your sure portion. God is faithful, God is faithful in preserving His people. "God is faithful, by whom you are called to the fellowship of His Son" (1 Corinthian 1:9). In the previous verse promise was made that God would confirm to the end His own people. The Apostle's confidence in the absolute security of believers was founded not on the strength of their resolutions or ability to persevere but on the honesty of Him that cannot lie. Since God has promised to His Son a certain people for His inheritance, to deliver them from sin and condemnation, and to make them participants of eternal life in glory, it is certain that He will not allow any of them to perish. God is faithful in disciplining His people. He is faithful in what He withholds, no less than in what He gives. He is faithful in sending sorrow as well as in giving joy. The faithfulness of God is a truth to be confessed by us not only when we are at ease, but also when we are sizzling under the sharpest rebuke. Nor must this confession be merely of our mouths, but of our hearts too. When God strikes us with the rod of chastisement, it is faithfulness which handles it. To acknowledge this means that we humble ourselves before Him, own that we fully deserve His correction, and instead of murmuring, thank Him for it. God never afflicts without reason. "For this cause many are weak and sickly among you" (1 Corinthian 11:30), says Paul, illustrating this principle. When His rod falls on us, let us say with Daniel, "O Lord, righteousness belongs to Thee, but to us confusion of faces" (9:7)" I know, O Lord, that Thy judgments are right and that Thou in faithfulness hast afflicted me" (Psalm 119:15). Trouble and affliction are not only consistent with God's love promised in the everlasting covenant , but they are parts of the administration of the same. God is not only faithful notwithstanding afflictions, but faithful in sending them.

[66]

"Thee will I visit their transgression with the rod, and their iniquity with stripes: My loving kindness, will I not utterly take from him nor suffer My faithfulness to fail" (Psalm 89:32, 33). Chastening is not only able to resolve differences with God's loving kindness, but it is the effect and the expression of it. It would much quite the minds of God's people if they would remember that His covenant love binds Him to lay on them seasonable correction.

Afflictions are necessary for us: "In their afflictions they will seek Me early" (Hosea 5:15). God is faithful in glorifying His people. "Faithful is He which calls you, who also will do" (1Thessalonians 5:24). The immediate reference here is to the saints being preserved blameless to the coming of our Lord Jesus Christ. God treats us not on the ground of our merits (for we have none), but for His own great name's sake. God is constant to Himself and to His own purpose of grace whom He called... them He also glorified (Romans 8:30). God gives a full demonstration of the constancy of His everlasting goodness toward His elect by effectually calling them out of darkness into His marvelous light, and this should fully assure them of the certain continuance of it. The foundation of God stands sure (2 Timothy 2:19). Paul was resting on the faithfulness of God when he said, I know whom I have believed, and am persuaded that He is able to keep that which I have committed to Him against that day (2 Timothy 1:12). The understanding of this blessed truth will preserve us from worry. To be full of care, to view our situation with dark gut feeling, to anticipate the morrow with sad anxiety, is to reflect upon the faithfulness of God. He who has cared for His child through all the years, will not forsake him in old age. He who has heard yours in the past, will not refuse to supply your need in the present emergency. Rest on Job 5:19, "He shall deliver thee in six troubles: yea in seven there shall be no evil touch thee." The Lord knows what is best for each of us, and one effect or resting on this truth will be the silencing of our irritable complaining. God is greatly honored when under trial and chastening, we have good thoughts of Him, vindicate His wisdom and justice, and recognize His love in His very rebukes.

The understanding of this blessed truth will create increasing confidence in God. "So then, those who suffer according to God's will should commit themselves to their faithful creator and continue to do good" (1 Peter 4:19). When we truthfully leave ourselves, and all our affairs into God's hands, fully persuaded of His love and faithfulness, the sooner shall we be satisfied with His providence and realize that "He does all things well."

Chapter Eight:
Smile, God Loves You

God's smile is upon you. You light up His face as much as anyone has ever lit up a sweetheart's face.

Most of us think that in God's eyes we are just one in a million. We know most people don't think we are important and so we assume God thinks of us in a similar way. But then again God is not like most people: We feel that God has favorites and we think we're somewhat way down the list, but we are about to see this is one way where feelings do not correspond to reality. To God, you are special, and you are God's favorite!

Four reasons why God favors no one over you

1. God's shed his last drop of blood for you. God loves you with his whole heart. He loves you with every bit of his enormous love. That means no matter how much he loves others, he couldn't possibly love anyone else more than he loves you.

You have asked the question: "God loves me with his whole heart? You got to be kidding! It's a wonder he loves me at all. This seems to be too much of an exaggeration." But the Lord will silence you when you read John 17:23:

[69]

"I in them and you in me. May they be brought to complete unity to let the world know

that you sent me and have loved them even as you have loved me."

When praying for all his followers including those who would believe later (verse 20) and Jesus declared that God loves them (me) just as passionately as God the Father loves his perfect, eternal Son.

We can't get around it. We can't dig under it or climb over it. So the only thing we can do is to go through it, absorbing it as we go. God has put it in black and white, and sealed it with the blood of his only Son that Christ is in us - and God loves us as much as He loves Christ. And no way can God 's love for Christ be half-hearted.

Scripture makes no promise that you will always feel loved, nor that circumstances will always make it obvious that you are loved. God simply promises that you are loved. No suffering or tragedy will ever separate you from God's love (Romans 8:35-39). A snap-shot in time proves nothing. Only eternity's moving picture can adequately portray the dynamics of God's love for you.

The more you love someone the more important that person is to you. So the fact that God loves you with his whole heart means you are more important to God than you could ever imagine or think.

2. Before God forgave us, we were all spiritually dead.
Scripture declares that every person on this planet was dead in

their sin. You can't get any deader than dead. God couldn't say I prefer her because she's a little less dead than him.

But through Christ we can be forgiven. When God looks at a forgiven person, he can't find one sin. When you are forgiven, God can't find a person on the entire planet more forgiven than you.

So without Christ we were all equally dead in our sin and in Christ we are all equally forgiven.

3. God is all-powerful. That means he doesn't need some people more than others.

If God can only use young people, or strong people, or rich people, or famous people, or educated people then God must be so weak that he needs human strength; poor that he needs us to give him a few dollars; so foolish that he needs human education.

4. The Lord loves using small and seemingly unimportant things. 1 Corinthians 1:26 says, "Look at what you were before God called you. Not many of you were wise by human standards. Not many of you had great influence. Not many of you came from important families. But God chose the foolish things of the world to shame the wise, and he chose the weak things of the world to shame the strong. He chose what this world thinks is unimportant and what this world looks down on and thinks is nothing in order to bring to nothing what the world thinks is important. God did this" the Bible continues, "so that no one could boast in his presence."

In the Bible, the book of Jonah seems small and insignificant. It's only 2-3 pages long. I often feel like that: small and insignificant. I have often felt so useless that I would have given up hope if I wasn't worried about having to face God afterwards. But the Bible would be very much poorer without this tiny book. And the kingdom of God would be much poorer without you. In this tiny book we see God using a storm, whale, a heartless, rebellious, moody man, a plant, and grub. Are you less gifted than a grub? Then God can do mighty things through you. If God could use a storm and a plant and a grub, God is smart enough to use you. God is so powerful he can use anything to do his work.

N0 Christian is too old, too poor, too uneducated, too stupid, too sick to be gloriously used of God.

Do you believe there is nothing God cannot do? Do you believe God could bring a dead person back to life through your prayers? Those words "through your prayers" don't suddenly make God weak. Do you believe God can save thousands of souls? Then you must also believe God can save thousands of souls through you.

Either God can do the impossible through you, or he isn't God.

Keep telling yourself, "There is nothing God cannot do through me."

Heaven waits on tip toe standing to see the astounding things you will achieve for the glory of God.

The decision

We now come to the most critical part of this chapter. This chapter could give you a lift for a few days, then fade and ultimately accomplish nothing. Or it could be the turning point in your life, making you the powerful force in the kingdom of God that you were created to be.

It's frightening to consider how much this world misses out when any Christian thinks he or she is not special to God. There's no Christian who cannot be used of God to win thousands of souls, should the Lord so chose. There's no Christian who can't be used to change the course of human history. But while we hold on to the sin of small thinking, it won't happen. This is serious - more serious than any of us can imagine. To rid ourselves of this sin will probably cost us enormously, but for us to be freed from sin cost Christ far more.

For us to give up the sin of small thinking is as hard as it is for an alcoholic to permanently give up drinking. We need a huge miracle in our personal lives. It begins by admitting that we are addicted to the serious sin of not seeing ourselves and our possibilities as God see them. We must hate this sin. We must admit that we are such a slave to this sin that the only way we can be freed is by a divine miracle.

Pray to God to open your mind and your conscience.

God loves you this much

The love of God is not based on what we have, what we do, or what we achieve in life. His vast love is not determined by our behavior, our attitude or our conduct. The love of God is not dependent on our personal background, our birth status, or our social standing. God's love is not influenced by anything that we do in and of ourselves. In all creation His love is like no other.

[73]

Romans 8:35-39 says, "For I am convinced that neither death nor life , neither angels nor demons, neither the present nor the future, nor any powers, neither height nor depth, nor anything else in all creation will be able to separate us from the love of God that is in Christ Jesus our Lord.

Wow, what a comfort, what a blessing, what joy there is in the love from our Lord to know that no hardships, troubles, lack of finances, nothing we can ever experience no matter how hard, trying or terrible things get, nothing can separate us from the love of God.

No hardship or distress we might encounter in life can be so overwhelming that God's love for you does not increase as what you are going through intensifies. At these moments His love grows strong. Such is not the human condition. There is no pain in life so powerful that God's love does not bring you comfort.

In life there may be times when you might experience hunger, but you will never be hungry for a lack of the Father's love. In life sometimes we are abandoned by those we love as financial dire situations plague us. But poverty and lack of finances cannot rob you of God's compassion, just as death itself is not capable of robbing us of our Father's infinite love.

Proverbs 3:11, 12 states, "My son, do not despise the Lord's discipline and do not resent his rebukes." Because the Lord disciplines those he loves, as a father, we are the children he delights in. As our heavenly Father, the love He gives and demonstrates toward us is 100% unconditional. Even if we are disobedient, get angry with God, follow our own will, He still loves us, even when we do not love Him in return. 1 John 4:19

[74]

tells us, "We love because He first loved us." His love for us as "Abba" our heavenly Father is so immeasurable and wide that he has made us heirs and has built a home for us in heaven and awaits the day when our flesh no longer remains, and we are as Paul writes, absent from the body, and present with the Lord. So these are things and definitions of our heavenly Father in the Bible.

He has adopted us and made us his children through the blood of his beloved Son Ephesians 1:5... he predestined us to be adopted as his sons through Jesus Christ, in accordance with his pleasure and will - God, "Abba" our heavenly Father desires an intimate relationship with us, his children. He is our comfort, and our strength. There are no arms bigger to hold you, and there is no love greater than His.

He alone is "Abba" dad, daddy, papa, and Father in every sense of the word. What a glorious blessing we have to have Him as our parent, and how precious and wonderful it is to be His child!

Chapter Nine:
The Meaning and
Importance of Faith

Many verses in the Scriptures deal with this important subject of faith. There is a whole chapter dedicated to it - Hebrews 11 - which describes men and women of faith and their acts of faith.

When we think about the subject of faith, many questions may arise: Does living faith mean believing in the unseen? Does it mean believing without good reason and acting without understanding? Isn't living by faith difficult and confusing? Why do we have to live our lives well without exercising faith?

In this chapter, we will search to understand what faith is, why it is important, and why living by faith is meaningful. Here, I am using "faith" in the essence of healthy, biblical faith - faith that God approves of.

Misconceptions about faith

Many regard faith as unexplainable, difficult to understand and hard to live by. There are many misconceptions. Let us think about some of these misconceptions.

Misconception #1 - How we feel indicates the quality of our faith

We often make the mistake of measuring our faith by how we feel. If we feel low, we think our faith is low and our life is in a poor state. If we feel high, we think our faith is high and our life is in good state. This is obviously an inadequate way of understanding our lives and the meaning of faith. Our spiritual health and our quality of our faith are not measured by our feelings.

Let us take notice of an event in the life of Jesus recorded in Matthew 26 -

Matthew 26:37, 38 - "And He took with Him Peter and the two sons of Zebedee and began to be grieved. (38) Then He said to them "My soul is deeply grieved, to the point of death; remain here and keep watch with me."

Here we see Jesus being grieved and distressed. It may seem that He was having a crisis of faith. But when we look at the next verse, we will see that this was not the case.

Matthew 26:39 - "And He went a little beyond them and fell on His face and prayed saying, "My Father if it is possible, let this cup pass from Me; yet not as I will, but as you will."

Despite being deeply grieved and distress, Jesus remained faithful and obedient to God the Father. He did not diminish from the horrible agonizing death on the Cross, but went through it victoriously.

Regard also the life of Apostle Paul. In his second letter to the Corinthians, he spoke much about the victorious Christian life. Some people think that the victorious life is one that transcends the human experience, where we are not subject to human emotions, not taxed or in distress. But this is far from the truth.

[77]

Notice how Paul describes in this letter his experience and that of his co-workers: "We were burdened excessively, beyond our strength, so that we despaired even of life" (2 Corinthians 1:8). He also tells us about their being tormented, confused, persecuted and struck down. Yet he also share with us how in the midst of the distresses, they were not crushed or despairing, not forsaken or destroyed (2 Corinthians 4:8, 9).

Obviously, in the case of Jesus and Apostle Paul though they were grieved and distressed, their lives were not in a poor state. On the contrary, they were able to live a triumphant life of faith under the most difficult circumstances.

So, let us not think that when we are feeling low, distressed, sad, or grieved over certain matters, it means our faith is of a poor quality. Conversely, let us not think that when we are feeling high, it means our faith our faith is strong and healthy. We may be feeling high, but the feeling may be superficial, emotional or temporary.

In the parable of the sower (Luke 8:4-15), Jesus tells the story of seed that fell on various kinds of ground. He compares the seed that fell on rocky soil to those who receive the word of God with joy, but after a time, fall away. Some people feel much joy when they become Christians and they are under the impression that their faith is very strong. After a while however, they find their walk with the Lord lacking in power and they become discouraged. They may wonder: Why this is happening to me? Why does my faith fluctuate so badly? Why do I feel so high one moment and so low the next? Why is my faith so strong one moment and so weak the next? Why has my life become so miserable all of a sudden? The truth of the matter is that their faith in the Lord has not been strong from the beginning, even when they were feeling high. Emotions are not a good measure of a person's faith.

Misconception #2 - Believing and acting on something we do not understand is expression of faith

Another conception is that we are exercising faith when we believe and act on something we do not understand. A person who cannot give a good or reasonable answer to the course of action he is taking may say, "I am doing this in faith." Because he thinks he is acting in faith does not mean that all will be well. The outcome can be tragic. Notice what happened to the Jewish exorcists in Acts 19:

Acts 19:13-16 - "But also some of the Jewish exorcists, who went from place to place, attempted to name over those who had the evil spirits the name of Jesus saying, "I adjure you by Jesus whom Paul preaches." (14) Seven sons of Sceva, a Jewish chief priest, were doing this. (15) And the evil spirit answered and said to them, I recognize Jesus, and I know about Paul, but who are you?" (16) And the man, in whom was the evil spirit, leaped on them and subdued all of them and overpowered them so that they fled out of that house naked and wounded.

These Jewish exorcists did not understand the workings of the spiritual realm. They thought they could exercise the same kind of power as Paul did just by using the name of Jesus over the evil spirits. But they met with an embarrassing and negative outcome. From this episode, we see that it does not mean when we do something we do not understand, we are doing it in faith.

Misconception #3 - Strong beliefs equal strong faith

[79]

Some people think that so long as they hope for something and believe very strongly in it, they are exercising faith. They misapply Hebrews 11:1: "Now faith is the assurance of things hoped for, the conviction of things not seen." They think that the more they believe in something, the stronger their faith is, and the more likely it will happen. But when they fail their examinations, they become discouraged, thinking that God has not honored their faith. Some, on the other hand, may think that they fail because they did not believe hard enough and they conclude that their faith was weak.

Misconception #4 - Doing something dangerous and risky is manifestation of faith

Some people associate faith with doing dangerous and risky things. Thus, if you have the nerve to row a small boat across a great ocean, or if you leave your comfortable home to serve God in a poorly developed country, they will say you have great faith. But is this how God looks at our lives? Is this how He commends us? Does it mean that the more difficult or riskier the thing we do, the stronger our faith is? This way of thinking is clearly defected. Quality of faith is not judged by how dangerous or risky the act is.

Misconception #5 - Sincerity is proof of faith

Even when we are sincere in the things we do, it does not guarantee that our actions would be acts of faith. We can be very sincere and be totally wrong. We may sincerely believe that we should act in a certain way, but we may be mistaken or deceived by the evil one. If we are mistaken or deceived, we would be acting in true faith. Belief in wrong doctrines can lead us astray. We can be sincere, yet influenced by wrong teaching. Having full confidence in something or someone does not mean that all will turn out well.

Several years ago my mother ended up in the hospital very ill. My sister and I fasted and prayed for our mother for several days. At the time, my sister and I trusted more in the fast and prayer. Yet, despite all we had done, our mother died. We sincerely believed all would turn out well for our mother. I saw my mother's death in a dream. I ignored what I saw. Sincerity is not proof of true faith.

What is true faith?

Having viewed the misconceptions of faith, let us ponder what true faith is. It is very important that we are clear about this issue as true faith is crucial for living a life pleasing to God.

Biblical faith has two crucial elements. First, it is belief in the truth. What we believe in must be based on facts, on what is true. Truth includes total reality, and total reality includes both the seen and the unseen realms. Belief in the truth in itself is, however, not true faith. There must be the second element: the appropriate response to the truth. In other words, we must be living out faith.

Such a life, that is, the life of true faith, would mean trusting God and obeying Him, believing in His word and living it out - for He is the God of truth and His word is truth. It would mean living according to what the Scriptures teaches and according to God's guidance. It is a life based on an accurate understanding of the Scriptures - who God is and what He has truly revealed. If we misapply the Scriptures or are deceived, we would not be exercising biblical faith.

[81]

The apostle Paul tells us this is the life of faith that God intends for all His children: "God has chosen you from the beginning for salvation through sanctification by the Spirit and faith in the truth" (2 Thessalonians 2:13). "Faith in the truth" in this context would mean the appropriate response of the heart to the accurate understanding of all that God has revealed in the Scriptures and to His will for our lives. This is the way for us to attain to all that God intends in salvation plan for us in Christ.

We must check the various concepts of faith that come to our mind against this understanding of true faith: Are there these two elements of true faith - believing in the truth and living in accordance with the truth?

True faith results in truly positive outcome

Hebrew 11 illustrates true faith in action. In the many examples of faith quoted, we see three aspects of true faith: First, knowing the truth; second, living the truth; and third, the positive outcome. The first two aspects are expressions of faith. The third shows us that ultimate, those who exercised true faith were not disappointed, for God rewarded them (v.6). God approved of their lives, and their expressions of faith had positive impact in God's kingdom. Let us examine the examples of Noah and Abraham.

Example of Noah

Hebrew 11:7 - "By faith Noah, being warned by God about things not yet seen, in reverence prepared an ark for the salvation of his household, by which he condemned the world, and became an heir of the righteous which is according to faith.

[82]

Noah was warned by God about things not yet seen. Faith can involve things we have not seen or which we do not fully understand.

Noah heard God and he responded by preparing an ark. His obedient action led to the salvation of his household and the announcement of the Scriptures that he was an heir of the righteousness which is according to faith.

Noah was commended for his faith not merely because he acted on something difficult and which he did not fully understand. He was commended because he acted on God's instruction.

Example of Abraham

Now, let us notice the life of faith in Abraham:

Hebrews 11:8 - "By faith Abraham, when he was called, obeyed by going out to a place which he was to receive for an inheritance; and he went out, not knowing where he was going.

Some people think that it is an act of faith to go forth when they do not know where they are going. But this in itself may not be a true act of faith. The crucial question is: Has God called? Abraham's going forth was an act of faith because he acted on God's call. Even if Abraham were prepared to take all kinds of risks, he would not have acted in true faith if God had not called him. Yes, Abraham did face many uncertainties - "he went out , not knowing where he was going." He could not fully comprehend what his action will lead to. Humanly speaking, there were risks involved. But one thing was clear to him, God had called. And Abraham trusted God and obeyed. That was a step of faith.

Besides trusting in God's call to go to a foreign land, Abraham also trusted in God's promise about his descendants (Romans 4:16-21).

Hebrew 11:12 - "Therefore there was born even of one man, and him as good as dead at that, as many descendents as the stars of heaven in number, and innumerable as the sand which is by the seashore.

Even though Abraham was old and incapable of producing a son, "him as good as dead" as the Scriptures put it, he trusted in God's promise of a son. Because of his faith in God, there was a positive outcome - Isaac was born and through him descendants as numerous as the stars of heaven. And so, Abraham is held up in the Scriptures as a shining example of a man of faith and he has a place of honor in God's kingdom.

As we can see from the examples of Noah and Abraham, faith is a response of our total being. It involves our mind in understanding, and our spirit in perceiving spiritual reality. It also involves our will in choosing. Unless we choose to respond appropriately to the truth we have come to understand, the response of faith is not yet complete.

Faith is a moral issue. It does not just descend upon us as a gift. That is why God approves of those who exercise faith. God does not praise us because we are gifted - whether in preaching, in teaching, in counseling, or other areas of life. God does not reward us for the fact that we have certain gifts because these are gifts He has given to us. When God praises us, when He approves of our lives, it is because of our good moral response. Though some people may not be able to understand very much with their mind, they can still become men of faith. God has His ways of helping us to recognize the truth. The critical matter at hand is whether there is hunger in our hearts to know the truth because we want to walk in truth and righteousness.

Acts of faith need not be spectacular or dangerous. A life of daily obedience to God, of trusting Him, of keeping His word; simple acts of love and kindness - these are expressions of a life of faith. At the heart of a life of faith is love for God, confidence in Him, and faithfulness to Him, the God of truth and righteousness.

Faith in the Scriptures

Biblical faith is never blind. It is not an abandonment of the mind. It does not hate knowledge or understanding. Rather, true faith builds upon the foundation of knowledge and understanding.   And just as a building rises above its foundation, a man of faith acts beyond what he can grasp and understand, but not in contradiction to it. So we can act with conviction on issues even when we do not fully understand them, so long as we know we are acting in accordance with God's will and instructions. This is because we know God is perfect and therefore absolutely dependable.

Abraham may not have fully understood the meaning and implications of God's instructions for him to go to another country, to take such a risky and dangerous step (humanly speaking), but it does not mean that when he went forth, he was acting in contradiction to the whole of what he was able to understand. He had already come to know God, and knew God loved him, cared for him and was dependable. So when God called him, he could go forth in faith.

[85]

This point is essential because communication between God and man is not perfect. There will be times when we are unclear whether a course of action is of God. What do we do then? At such times, we need to examine carefully by considering the relevant factors, especially if the issues are significant. If we think that the course of action may be contrary to scriptural principles, we should pause. We should not follow through with a course of action that we recognize to be contrary to the fundamental principles we have already come to understand. But, we need not act only when we are able to understand fully. In other words, faith is not blind. It builds upon understanding and knowledge and does not contradict them.

It is important that we know what true faith is - the kind that God approves of. A belief based on falsehood is useless. We need to grow in understanding of the truth and have a deep desire to abide by it. Otherwise, the knowledge we gain will be useless to us and there will be no true faith. We need to recognize that faith is so important to our lives. We need to constantly live our lives taking into consideration the whole reality in both the visible and the invisible realms. In fact, we need to recognize the realm of the unseen. God is invisible, and many important aspects of our lives on earth take place in the realm of the unseen and involve issues we may not fully understand.

Let us not, because of our lack of faith, hinder God from working in and through our lives. Let us nurture our love for the truth and deepen our commitment to live by it. Let us seek to grow in our knowledge of God and His ways so that we can respond well and live out the life of fullness God intends for us in Christ.

[86]

Chapter Ten:
When God Says No

There are times when we start to pray, and we have no idea what to pray for. There are times when we just don't know what to say to God. But, we can rest secured that God understands us, and knows what we need. We can be sure that He is going to answer our prayers. There are too many believers out there who believe that there are times when God doesn't answer their prayers. We need to grasp that there's no such thing as "unanswered prayer." We can see very clearly when a prayer is answered "yes" by God. But, there are times when God may reply by saying "wait," because we need to wait for the answer. And, there are other times when God says "no." Let's look at what happens when God says no. Does that show that God does not care for us? Does it mean that He's being heartless? Let's examine a couple of different times in Scripture when God said no to His children's prayers.

I. Paul's Thorn in the Flesh

A. 2 Corinthians 12:7-10a God very clearly said no to Paul. It appears that this thorn in the flesh which has been thought to be numerous different things, stayed with him possibly until his death. Why did God let Paul suffer from such ailment? Why did God deliberately allow Paul to endure pain? "My grace is sufficient for you, for power is perfected in weakness." We can learn from the Lord in this statement.

B. First, God says, "my grace is sufficient for you." God is telling Paul that he doesn't need to worry about this thorn in the flesh because God's grace has freed his soul. God reminds Paul that while there are going to be things on this earth that will cause a great deal of physical pain, yet, we can still know that God has given us His Son to take away our spiritual punishment.

God says, "No, I'm not going to remove this physical ailment because life isn't supposed to be free of pain. But, you can rely on me to relieve your spiritual pain.

C. Secondly, God says, "power is perfected in weakness." What kind of power are we to think God is concerned with here? He just reminded Paul that he should be more concerned with his spiritual health than his physical well-being. So, obviously we can see that God is focused on spiritual power. So how is spiritual health perfected in weakness? Think about it for a moment before you answer.

When do we pray the most? Do we pray a lot more when we're happy, and things are going our way, and the sun is shining, and we've got no worries? The answer is No, we don't. We pray more when we're suffering; when we've got major problems; when we don't know what to do. God is saying to Paul, and to us today, that when we are weakened by this life, that's when we are the strongest because that's when we start to rely more on the Lord. That's when we start to pray wholeheartedly to Him.

How many stories have you heard people tell about a time in their life when things were going great, and they just decided to start praying more, and everything just got even better? I don't

[88]

remember ever hearing a story like that. But, on the other hand, I have heard many stories of people whose lives were in disarray, and they decided to turn to God, and when they did, everything changed. It doesn't mean that they were miraculously healed, or completely freed of their situations, but they knew that God was in control, and they began to rely on Him.

II. Jesus in Gethsemane

A. Our next example comes from Luke 22:39-44a We know that God said no to this prayer. Jesus prayed that He wouldn't have to go through so much suffering. But, God said no. There are two important things for us to recognize about this interaction here.

B. First, we need to notice how this prayer was prayed. How often do we actually pray words like, "not my will, but yours be done?" Usually, it's like, "Lord, I need this, and I need it now." We have a disposition to see God not as someone we bring our requests to, but rather like we go up to the counter and order what we want, and if we don't get it, we get upset. Is that the way prayer works? Of course not! We shouldn't expect God to be at our beckon call. God isn't there just to fix whatever we have a problem with in our lives. God is the creator of this world, and He is going to allow things to progress as He sees fit, not as I demand.

C. Secondly, Let's take a close look at God's answer to this prayer. Yes, God says no to Jesus. Jesus desires to be freed from the unavoidable suffering he was going to have to face, but God said no. The important lesson for us is that we need to realize how much more God knows than us. A lot of times we

[89]

approach God thinking we know what's best for us. But, we will learn very quickly that the Lord knows best.

D. Perhaps we should be a little less demanding when it comes to our prayer life. We all could use a little more humility in our prayers, and we should become well familiarized with the phrase "not my will, but yours be done."

III. God's Answer to Job

A. Lastly, let's look at Job 40:10-14. Job hasn't been practicing his attitude of "not my will, but yours be done." Job has been demanding an answer for why he has suffered so much. He feels that God owes him an explanation. Have you ever felt this way? Have you ever entered prayer as though you were raising your fists in anger toward God? Is it such a surprise that with an attitude like that, that God would say no?

B. God says to Job, "If you are so great of a being that you can question me, then you will be able to make the proud humble. You will be able to bring down judgment on all the wicked." God is saying that He is in charge here. Furthermore, He's saying, "Don't you realize that you're not the one in control here?"

C. God also points out something very important for us to remember. In verse 14, God said that if Job can do all these things he has listed, then He will admit that Job can save himself. This, of course, is absurd. We know that Job couldn't save himself. None of us can save ourselves. We must rely on the grace and forgiveness of the Father. So why do we pray as though we are the ones in control? Why do we pray as though we are the one who make the decisions? We need to remember

[90]

to approach God's throne with fear and respect for who He is, and what He can do for us.

IV. Real prevailing prayer must have your very best offering of self and substance wrapped up in it. A. When you pray for the relief of the poor, is your prayer anything more than words? When you insistently instruct the Lord to convert the unbeliever, are there any heartless words wrapped up in your prayer?

B. When we pray, is there any substance to it? Or do we expect God to do everything for us? Sometimes, we may think God has said no to our requests, when in actuality, He's said, "here's your opportunity to take care of it" and we let it slip by. Let's make sure, first of all, that we are coming to God with the right attitudes when we pray.

C. God is going to deny our requests from time to time. But, we have to remember that there is a reason behind it. Whether it's because it will make us strong, or because He knows of better options that we can't foresee. If we will come to God humbly, and with some substance to our prayers, then we are much more likely to have a successful prayer life. But, we need to remember the saying, "Prayer doesn't get our will done in heaven, but God's will done on earth."

The following is a beautiful poem to read when you are discouraged:

All of your days have already been written in God's book.

When you go through a disappointment, don't stop on that page.

[91]

Stay the course. Keep believing. You may be tired, discouraged and frustrated,

but don't give up on your future, Our God is faithful.

Chapter Eleven:
This is Not the
Time to Quit

Some days do you just want to give up? Perhaps, you are wearied of trying and, in all probability, you're spinning in circles and going nowhere. You may even notice other people less deserving getting ahead, and you're stuck in the same place.

Life might have gotten tiresome. Feelings of incompetency leak into your mind. Or, a disappointment has caused you to fall back into old, destructive patterns. Now, you could be off track, dishearten and your energy may be drained.

But wait. You matter. Your life counts. No matter what you are going through today, God has not given up on you, so don't you dare give up on yourself. Decide now to get off the fast track of negative thoughts and begin to see beyond the present moment. God has a marvelous plan and place for you. And your future holds great promise.

Years ago, I experienced a huge road blocked in my life, where I was so discouraged that I wanted to relinquish my hopes, dreams for the future and just give up on life. I planned to leave the church, relationships and abandon my walk with God, settling for the status quo.

But before quitting, I decided to speak with a very dear friend of mind before making such an important decision. Before meeting with my dear friend, I went to visit my mother, as usual, on Saturdays to see how she was doing. Immediately, she noticed that something was very wrong with me. I did not look like my usual jolly self with a big smile. She asked me several questions, but, I had very few answers for her since I didn't know the answers myself. However, my mother came up with this brilliant idea for me to take a trip to the Caribbean for one week. I had the choice to go to the Virgin Island, California, or Florida.

Because I've done very little traveling, I really didn't know which place to choose. All I knew is that I needed to get away. So my mother suggested for me to go to the Virgin Island since my grandmother travelled there and love it. So I agreed. Then my mother purchased two tickets for the Virgin Island, one for my sister and one for me since she did not want me to travel alone.

About a week before my trip to the Virgin Island, I made an appointed to speak with my friend. During our meeting, I learned that I was tying God's hand, and that He was waiting on me. This was a rude awakening for me because I was blaming God for all my unhappiness. After the meeting, my dear friend encourage me to go on the trip and to enjoy myself. I had a blast. It was exactly what I needed! This trip changed my life forever. During this trip, I met my beloved husband.

[94]

It doesn't matter how impossible your circumstance appears to be or how long it takes, your time of victory will come. You will climb high. You will blossom. So don't quit, and give God the glory, by climbing as high as you can.

The day I left the Caribbean and slowly made my way back home, I did not feel the same about my heavenly Father. With my head held high, and a renewed strength, I felt surrounded by God's love. I realized that God would never give up on me. And, dear brothers/sisters, God will never give up on you, either.

Your life is full of countless possibilities. You have too much yet to do, too many lives to positively impact upon and too many dreams to discover to quit now. Your season of victory, too, is coming. So whatever may be troubling you, turn it all over to God and move forward. There is no obstacle too big for God to turn around for your greater good. He is working right now in your behalf and is "going before you and making the crooked places straight." (Isaiah 45:2-3).

Therefore, continue in faith and say, "I am not going to give up. I'm moving forward with God," and "I'll become all that God intends for me to be." God has not brought you this far to leave you here. He is about to do something greater than you can ever imagine. So, continue your pursuit. Don't stop now. And keep on going.

In the Bible, I read about the Prodigal Son. A father had two sons and the younger son requested of his father to give him his portion of his inheritance early, from the family estate. The father granted his request and the young son went off to distant lands and begins to waste his inheritance in wild living. A famine hits the country, the young son's money runs out, and he finds himself impoverished, in horrible conditions. Finally, the young son comes to his senses and although unsure of the welcome he'd receive, returns home.

Upon seeing his son, the father who had been watching and waiting for him, ran out to greet his beloved son with opened arms and rejoiced that the son found his way back home. (Luke 15:11-32).

Nothing could separate the son from his father's love, and nothing can separate you from God's love. So, persevere onward, under God's love, guidance and care. Then watch in astonishment as He blesses all areas of your life. And peace, joy and victory will be yours.

Remain faithful. Stay calm. Persevere

As Christians, we are aware we cannot descend from grace, but we do descend into grace. God's grace is an undeserved, unmerited present to the believer and thankfully. God never go back on following through on His present to those who truly believe.

What can we do to stay faithful to our God who loves us so freely and generously? We can aim to be informed, connected and involved. Jude 1:17-25 tells believers how to remain faithful in their walk with the Lord. The chapter concludes with God's inspiring promise to keep us safely by His side.

Read Jude 1:17-25.

First, Jude encourages us to be informed (v. 19). When you notice those who cause division in the body or set themselves up above the Word of God, be on guard. Don't be taken in by smooth talk or new twists. Don't accept anything as a substitute for grace. Test everything by the Word of God.

Secondly, take measures to insulate yourself against unbelief. " Build yourself up in your most holy faith" (v. 20). Devote the time it takes to develop closeness with God's Word. Books and sermons cannot take the place of time reading the Bible.

Remain with God in prayer. Do not let anything, or even good things like family or ministry, to take the place of time with God. If you ignore Him, you will find yourself spiritually dry. You will not lose your salvation, but you may miss out on some of God's blessings.

When the prodigal son wandered away from his father, he did not lose the father's love, but he suffered. He missed out on the many blessings of living closely and intimately with his father. The prodigal forfeited the joy of daily experiencing his father's love. When you spend time away from the Father, what effects does that have on you, your emotions, or your choices!

Also, insulate yourself from those who knew truth but have turned their backs on it (1 Corinthians 5:12-13). Instead, Jude says in verse 22 to get involved with non-believers "Be merciful to those who doubt." Do not angrily preach the truth, but show them the same mercy and love Christ did. Prayerfully speak the truth in love.

Is your heart moved by thee many unsaved in the world around you? Are you involved?

Jude's epistle concludes with the best part, God's part in keeping us safe. Verses 24-25 offer an uplifting description of what God stands ready to do for believers. "To him who is able to keep you from falling and to present you before his glorious presence without fault and with great joy - to the only God our Savior be glory, majesty, power and authority, through Christ our Lord, before all ages, now and forevermore."

What is worrying you today? Your health or finances? Politics or breaking news? A relationship with a family member? A lost friend? The Lord will sustain you in your circumstances. Your hand is in God's hand. Like the good father He is, He will not let you go.

Remember that Jesus said in John 6:39 that it is "the will of him who sent me, that I shall lose none of all that he has given me, but raise them up at the last day." One day, He will present you to His Father in Heaven. Until then, He will see you all the way home.

Praise the Lord for the promise He gave you for your future with Him in Heaven and for the protection and companionship that is yours now as you walk out your faith.

Chapter Twelve:
The King Wants to
Bring You Out

Believers now have authority in Christ over all hindrances from the enemy. Through Jesus you are more than a conqueror because He has overcome the world. You just need to believe that He can and will be with you in all of your situations. Your failures do not stop His love and your problems can never hinder His perfect plan for your life. His birth symbolized a pledge to bring you peace no matter what you may be going through. Jesus is the Word made flesh and the light of this world who will never let you down. He willingly left the brilliance of heaven to come to this earth knowing that we would reject Him. Yet His love was so great that He chose to walk with us and be crucified to bring us peace with the Father and spend eternity with Him forever.

The peace He promised to leave us is sufficient to meet any need and to take you through any storm in your life. His power is strong enough to safely take you though all circumstances and to give you joy in the midst of your storm. He knew your name and loved you long before you were born. He has plans to prosper you and give you a future despite your short comings. He is faithful to make a way for you even when the door is closed. Most importantly, He will never leave you to carry your burden alone. In Matthew 28:20, Jesus says,

"And surely I am with you always, even to the very end of the age."

Your situation is never futile when you have Christ in your heart. He is able to heal any sorrow or hurt you may have and give you the confidence that His love will comfort you in your pain. He is the source of your strength and the power to restore you in all ways. His gift of life is free for the asking. His love will never fail you and His peace will keep you as you focus your attention only on Him. Take heart and be encouraged.

Get ready for testing!

We are living in the last days. God is allowing believers to be shaken to their core beyond their own strength to find out who truly belongs to Christ. It is for that reason that you must stand your ground and let God do His work of refining you for an eternal kingdom.

In 2 Corinthians, Chapter 1, we read that Paul suffered through depression as he spread the gospel. He says in verse 8-9, "For we do not want you to be unaware brothers, of the affliction we experienced in Asia. For we were so utterly burden beyond our strength that we despaired of life itself. Indeed, we felt that we had received the sentence of death. But that was to make us rely not on ourselves but on God who raises the dead." Even the apostle Paul had to suffer for Christ to the point of wanting to give up and die. How much more are we struggling in the last days as Christ is coming quickly to take us from this immoral earth? Without missing a beat the enemy has stepped up his game as he initiates attacks from all sides upon believers who are shining the light of the kingdom to the lost.

We should not be amazed that we are facing trials of every kind. While the enemy wants to destroy us with his lies and deception we are being affirmed to be warriors of wrath in the army of the living God. In the book of James, the disciple tells us that the testing of our faith produces a steadfastness which God is perfecting in us so that we will lack nothing of worth. Have no doubt that God's argels are surrounding you at this moment. They are ministering to you in your heartache and strengthening you during your fears. They have been given orders from the Throne of God to guard your pathway to Him. You cannot be conquered.

As the earth gives way to the enemy's lies, we agonize through financial problems, sickness and disease, marriages failing, addictions and all forms of bondage as danger creeps on every corner. We cannot escape the battle launched by the spiritual forces of darkness; however, believers are guaranteed victory through it all.

Those who submit to God and resist the deception of this world have hope that eternity with God will be a reward that will last forever. Don't let your painful trials to make you take your focus from the truth. You need to understand that your purpose in God's plan has been set before the foundations of the world. You cannot be shifted from your position by the slingshots and arrows of the enemy. You will never be taken down. Surrender your weariness to the One who always has your back through your problems. He can lift you above them all and hold onto you until He has filled you with His peace.

The deceiver wants you to forget that your destiny has been sealed by the blood of Christ. Stay strong and don't lose sight of the blessed hope which never fails. Pick up your shield and let the armor of God be your protection. Nothing of value can ever be taken from you in this fallen world. You have been guaranteed a royal future. The book of life has your name in it. What can flesh do to you?

This message is for Christians. It is the truth from God's word that He will always be with us in everything and through all the storms we face. We are never alone. We are being sifted like wheat by the enemy but Christ is with us so that we will not fail. No matter what you are going through, it is being viewed by the eyes of God. You're not alone and never without hope.

The blessed truth is that there is a perfect plan unraveling for those who refuse to be removed from their position in Christ. You may feel like you are too overwhelmed to continue in the battles you face, but the power of God is always the conquering force within you in all your hardships. There is not a moment that your future is ever compromised by issues in your life. You have been given the guarantee of victory in all situations. God is working divine, eternal destiny through every single one of them.

In Isaiah 40:31 reads, "but they who wait for the Lord shall renew their strength; they shall mount up with wings like eagles." Those who can trust that God is still sovereign in their darkest test and hurt shall not go unrewarded. He will give you the power and hope you need to stay in the race and not give up. It was by His grace that you were taken this far and He

[102]

will not let you be destroyed now. Surrender your fears and frustrations to God and let Him give you His peace to endure.

It may seem like your prayer has not been answered or that your issue is getting worse but the God who calls out each star by name without losing one is certainly not going to lose you during any battle that you face. You are a winner and your destiny is sealed. Don't allow your pain to weaken your faith in the heavenly Father. There is always the hope you need to carry on for your steps are guided by the hand of God. Lift up your eyes to the hills from whence comes your help. Hold on. Your Father sees where you are and He will rescue you.

Unfortunately, for quite some time I have been living with the pain of a failing marriage. Despite doing all that I could, it is obvious that I cannot change the outcome.. Although I have been praying night and day for God's strength and guidance, things have gotten worse. All I can do now is to continue to pray and surrender my will to Christ. He alone knows the outcome. It breaks my heart to realize that I cannot make someone stay and love me when he has chosen not to. I feel betrayed and hurt facing an uncertain future. But as difficult as this has been for me, I know that God still has a plan for my life.

I want to make it very clear that God has authority over all that we face. He can and will do mighty things to help His people and that is why I advise those struggling in failing marriages to pray and not give up. I am still praying for all who are going through troubled marriages. We have good reason to hope that God can reach the unbelieving spouse. Sometimes He takes them to the end of their rope (strength) so that they have nowhere to turn but to Him. However, I know it is hard to understand the times when that doesn't happen. It does not mean that God doesn't care. The truth is that He cares much and He grieves with us in our struggle. Unfortunately, we are living in a lost and perishing world and the enemy has blinded most to his schemes. His main target is to break up homes and destroy families supported by the fact that over half of all marriages end in divorce. What a sad statistic that is. Yet God still has the power to give you a future with hope.

When you do all that you can and it seems like you are being hard pressed on every side, remember that in Christ, you cannot be crushed. He will take your broken heart and your fallen dreams and use them to build you up for His purpose. It may seem like you will never recover from your pain or that your tears will never end, but that is not true. King David wrote in Psalm 69 "Save me, O God! For the waters have come up to my neck, I sink in the deep mire, where there is no foothold; I have come into deep waters and the flood sweeps over me. I am weary with my crying out; my throat is parched. My eyes grow dim with waiting for my God." And yet David kept trusting his God even when all hope seemed irretrievable.

The good news is that our problems and struggles do not dictate our future. It is planned out by Christ who will not fail to help those who trust in Him. I know that my pain has no power to destroy the hope I have through Christ. Despite what I face in this life, my God will always be bigger.

Nothing happens apart from His knowledge and permission. Each day, the enemy wants me to believe that God has failed me or that He doesn't care. He tries to convince me that I am alone. Yet, I know by faith that I will never be alone. Psalm 23 reminds us that, "Even though I walk through the

[104]

valley of the shadow of death, I will fear no evil, for you are with me." All of our enemies, our struggles and our pain has been rendered powerless to destroy us. Jesus has a way to heal and make us whole no matter how broken we are. I trust Him. Nothing is impossible for Him. If you can keep trusting Him despite your struggle, you will not be conquered. You will have the victory in everything even through the pain.

Chapter Thirteen: Un-forgiveness is Spiritual Bondage

Un-forgiveness is the single most sought after venom that the enemy uses against God's children, and it is one of the most terminal venom an individual can take spiritually. It effects everything from mental depression, to health problems such as cancer and arthritis. I'm not implying that every single case of cancer, it is because of un-forgiveness, but I am saying that it can cause cancer. Cancer comes from the devil, scientist is unable to explain it, doctors don't comprehend where it comes from; it's the signs of a curse. God allowed the Israelites to face diseases and sickness when they disobeyed Him (Deuteronomy 28:58-61), and when they decided to return to Him, He would heal their land and take sickness from their midst (Exodus 23:25, Deut. 7:15). On the other hand, in the New Testament, Jesus gave us two commandments (Matthew 22:37-40), and if we break these, we can be opened up to curses (called consequences), just like the people in the Old Testament were. Jesus never came to eliminate the law (Matthew 5:17) but He did come to deliver us from the curse of the law (Galatians 3:13), meaning, Jesus paid the full price so we can be delivered from any curses we may have come under.

Two commandments God gave us

Matthews 22:37-40, "Jesus said unto him, Thou shall love the Lord thy God with all thy heart, and with all thy soul, and with all thy mind. This is the first commandment. And the second is like unto it, Thou shall love thy neighbor as thyself. On these two commandments hang all the laws and the prophets."

Jesus gave us very significant commandments to follow; one of them was to love one another, as He has loved us (John 15:12). Love is the exact opposite of un-forgiveness, envy, jealousy, hate, resentment, pride and bitterness. You are unable to truly love somebody and hold bitterness or un-forgiveness against him or her at the same time.

Our responsibility to forgive others

God sent His Son Jesus to die for our sins, so that we may be rectified to Him, without spot or blemish. He asks that we give others the same forgiveness that paid for us. He tells a parable in Matthew 18:23-35 that says, "Therefore is the kingdom of heaven likened unto a certain king, which would take account of his servants. And when he had began to reckon, one was brought unto him, which owed him ten thousand talents. But forasmuch as he had not to pay, his lord commanded him to be sold, and his wife, and children, and all that he had and payment to be made. The servant therefore fell down, and worshipped him, saying, Lord have patience with me, and I will pay thee all. Then the lord of that servant was moved with compassion, and loosed him, and forgave him the dept. But the same servant went out, and found one of his fellow servants, which owed him an hundred pence: and he laid hands on him, and took (him) by the throat, saying Pay me that thou owe. And his fellow servant fell down at his feet, and besought him, saying, Have patience with me, and I will pay thee all. And he

[107]

would not: but went and cast him into prison, till he should pay the debt. So when his fellow servants saw what was done, they were very sorry, and came and told unto their lord all that was done. Then his lord, after that he had called him, said unto him, O thou wicked servant, I forgave thee all that debt, because thou desired me: Should not you also have had compassion on your fellow servant, even as I had pity on you? And his lord was angry, and delivered him to the tormentors, till he should pay all that was due to him. So likewise shall my heavenly Father do also to you, if you from your hearts forgive not everyone his brother their trespasses."

Un-forgiveness shows we don't really love Jesus

In John 15:12, Jesus expects us to love one another, as He has loved us. True love doesn't hold a grudge or un-forgiveness against that individual. If we are holding a grudge or un-forgiveness against somebody, then we don't love them as Christ loved us. If we don't keep Jesus' commandments, then it reveals we don't love Him.

Un-forgiveness stops God from forgiving our sins

Matthew 6:15 says, "But if you forgive not men their trespasses, neither will your Father forgive your trespasses."

Un-forgiveness exposes us to the tormentors (the devil)

Matthew 18:23-35, See the above.

Un-forgiveness can keep God from answering our prayers

Mark 11:24, 25 says, "Therefore I say to you, what thing so ever you desire, when you pray, believe that you receive them, and you shall have them. And when you stand praying, forgive, if you have ought (something) against any: that your Father also which is in heaven may forgive you your trespasses."

Matthew 7:7, 12 tells us, "Ask, and it shall be given you; seek, and you shall find; knock, and it shall be opened to you... Therefore all things whatsoever you would that men should do to you, do you even so to them..."

John 15:5, 10 tells us that if we abide in Christ, we will produce much spiritual fruit, and the way that we abide in Christ is by keeping His commandments. Verse 12 tells us that His commandment is to love one another as He has loved us. Verse 7 tells us that if we abide in Him (by keeping His commandments), and His Word in us, we can ask for anything and it will be given unto us. The reason that many people's prayer go unanswered, is because they aren't keeping the commandments that Jesus gave us; therefore they aren't abiding in Christ's love, and if we aren't abiding in Christ's love, how can we expect Him to hear our prayers?

Un-forgiveness can defile a person

Hebrews 12:15 states,... lest any root of bitterness springing up trouble you, and thereby many be defiled."

Pay attention to the end it says, "many be defiled." This is very common, if not one of the most common daily things that defile people. Many bondages can be loosed when a person forgives those who have wronged him or her.

Un-forgiveness can give Satan an advantage

2 Corinthians 2:10-11 states, "To whom ye forgive anything, I forgive also; for if I forgave anything, to whom I forgave it, for

your sakes forgave I it in the person of Christ; Lest Satan should get an advantage of us: for we are not ignorant of his devices."

Un-forgiveness can keep an individual out of heaven

Matthew 7:21 states, ..."Not everyone that says to me, Lord, Lord, shall enter into the kingdom of heaven; but he that does the will of my Father which is in heaven."

1 John 3:14 states, "We know that we have passed from death to life, because we love the brethren. He that loves not his brother abides in death."

Un-forgiveness can expose us to curses

When individuals in the Old Testament disobeyed God's commandments, it exposed them to curses (Deut. 27:26). When individuals nowadays choose to disobey God, it can do the same thing. Curses can cause mental and emotional dilemmas (Deut. 28:28), physical dilemmas (Deut. 28:35, 60, 61), financial dilemmas (Deut. 28:17, 38, 43), divorce and unfaithful spouse (Deut. 28:30, 56), emotional stress (Deut. 28:34), childlessness (Lev. 20:21), and that's not all, plus those curses can be handed down to your future generations (Exodus 20:5).

The blessings of forgiveness

When we forgive, it expose us to God's forgiveness (Matthews6:15), it puts us in a receiving mode when we pray (Mark 11:24, 25), it helps us become spiritually fruitful (John 15:5, 10, 12), and we will know that we have passed from spiritual death to being reconciled with our heavenly Father when we love each other (1 John 3:14). When we keep God's

[110]

commandments and love one another, we show that we love Jesus (John 14:21), and we abide in Christ's love (John 15:10). What a glorious blessing forgiveness offers us!!!

The power of forgiveness

The power to forgive is an unbelievably powerful and self-liberating precept which when consciously applied, allows a sense of in describable peace and overall well being to flow and penetrate your inner most being resulting in far greater and more pleasing outcomes in your physical world.

The consequence of starting this unbelievably power cannot be understated and can be much more easily understood by developing the consciousness and understand of how our universe operates in its precise, and perfectly constructed manner.

First of all let's examine the definition of forgiveness so that you might gain a better understanding of what true forgiveness really is.

According to the Merriam Webster to forgive is...

A) to give up resentment of, or claim to requital for B) to grant relief from payment of 2) to cease to feel resentment against (an offender) : Pardon intransitive senses: to grant forgiveness.

By developing a basic understanding of what you are creating by holding resentment, or failing to give up your claim to or refusal to grant relief of the offender, you will have the ability to make an educated and conscious choice as to your future actions with respect to forgiveness and the limitless power which is unleashed as a result of choosing to do so.

[111]

By continually and deliberately exercising your ability to forgive, you will begin to understand and experience the true and life transforming power of forgiveness in your physical outcomes and will have discovered the ability to allow unlimited and positive creative energy to continually flow in and through your life that is in harmony and alignment and with all that you desire and deserve to experience.

Although that I understand to an extent that forgiveness can appear difficult for some at times, utilizing and implementing the power of forgiveness, regardless of the circumstances is well within your ability to implement if you make the deliberate choice to do so. The power realized from doing so (or not) can mean the difference between a life of ease, harmony and overall well being or a life of hardship, conflict and illness.

These results whether perceived as good or bad do not happen as many perceive due to any form of wrath or judgment, but rather unfold due to a perfectly constructed and never changing process of creation based on unconditional love enabling us to experience life as we choose.

A choice to forgive or not is a choice that we have been provided the inalienable right of free will to exercise.

As has been shared by many doctors, psychologists, scientists, clergy etc., at the root of the majority of illness and disease, there lies a deeply embedded issue of un-forgiveness, at either on a conscious or unconscious level.

I have heard many individuals say that "My un-forgiveness is justified," and from human outlook, although many may agree with them, I can assure you that a refusal to forgive, regardless of the situation will certainly have an undesirable and negative effect on your outcomes in life whether physical, relationally, emotionally, and spiritually.

It is a little known fact that when someone makes a choice to hold resentment or un-forgiveness against another, they are not hurting the individual that they are holding the resentment against, but instead only hurting themselves.

It has been long understood and proven that a prolonged state of bitterness can have many negative side effects on the individual that harbors and holds on to resentment has proven to cause undesirable conditions, not only emotionally but physically as well.

Although the most commonly thought of form of forgiveness is in forgiving others that you have perceive have wronged you in some way, equally as important is developing the ability to forgive yourself for what you might perceive to be past mistakes that you have made, and which many choose to hold on to resulting in feelings of guilt.

Judge not and you will not be judge

Unconditional love and forgiveness is the nature of our Source (Creator) whatever you may perceive that to be. By developing the ability to forgive and eliminate judgment unconditionally, you will have made tremendous and powerful progress in your ability to begin experiencing a life of ease, harmony and overall well being physically, financially, relationally, emotionally and spiritually.

if you seem to struggle with the ability to forgive yourself or others, it is most certainly effecting your outcomes

[113]

in life and hopefully you now have a deeper understanding as to why and how.

Developing a discerning awareness of the importance of the power of forgiveness in your life, combined with the deeper understanding and correct implementation of that knowledge with focused intent, will empowering you to begin experiencing what you may have previously perceived as miracles to occur.

Don't pray the following prayer until you are ready to forgive the individual(s) who hurt you. It must be prayed from the heart.

Prayer to forgive others

Heavenly Father, in the name of Jesus, I thank you because you are holy and righteous. You are perfect in justice. I confess that I have not forgiven as you have commanded me to. Through Jesus Christ, I now forgive these people:_____(list names and what they did to you). I confess my pride and judgment against these people. Please forgive me Lord and cleanse me from my sin of un-forgiveness in my heart. Please help me to thoroughly cast these people and wrongs they caused me upon you. I pray that your will be done in my life and their lives. Please help me to forget those wrongs, but instead to focus my attention on you. I invite you, Father, into any painful memories I have concerning what was done. Please heal any wounds my soul has suffered and help me to have your perspective on this matter. Thank you, Father. In the name of Jesus I pray, Amen. (Now receive and praise the Lord for what He has done).

Chapter Fourteen: Arising Above Disappointment

Do you ever sense like God is not there? Although our emotions tells us that at times, we should not be controlled by our emotions when it comes to our confidence in God. Since Scriptures states, the "righteous shall live by faith" (Romans 1:17) and "without faith it is impossible to please God" (Hebrews 11:6), we should not require to feel God to know He is there. But I can relate to how you feel if you find yourself disappointed at times, because it appears like God just is not around.

Unanswered prayer, a series of discouraging events, or a betrayal by someone close to you can cause you to believe that God has checked out of your life. Other times we get too busy with our day-to-day lives that we feel condemned that we are not doing enough for God to want to be around us. But since God has promised He will never leave us or forsake us (Hebrews 13:5), we can be certain of His constant presence whether we are struggling with a painful event or just too busy to observe He is near.

Here are seven ways to center on Him and sense His presence in the middle of your battle or your disordered schedule:

1. Come Clean with Him. Sometimes you cannot feel God's presence because there is something obstructing communication between the two of you. He has not left, but your responsiveness to His presence might be affected by unconfessed sin in your life. David, the Psalmist said, "When I kept silent (concerning his sin) my bones wasted away through my groaning all day long. For day and night your hand was heavy upon me; my strength was sapped as in the heat of summer. Then I acknowledged my sin to you and did not cover up my iniquity. I said, "I will confess my transgressions to the Lord" - and you forgave the guilt of my sin" (Psalms 32:3-5). If you sense God is not around because the two of you have not spoke in a while, or because you have refrained or shun the thought of Him for so long, confess to God what is on your heart and mind and ask Him to give you an ear to hear His voice again. 1 John 1:9 tells us; "If we confess our sins, He is faithful and righteous to forgive us our sins and to cleanse us from all unrighteousness." When your fellowship with Him is restored, the communication can flow again. So take the time to get clean, through the forgiveness of Christ, and allow it to flow.

2. Read Scripture Aloud. When you audibly speak God's inspired Word, you will feel its power and His presence. The Bible says God's Word is "living and active and sharper than any two-edged sword" (Hebrews 4:12). That sharp sword will either make you aware of its weight or prick your heart through faith, prompting, and perseverance. A pricked heart is better off than a duel heart any day, wouldn't you agree?

3. Sing Him a Love Song. God inhabits the praises of His people. Did you ever wonder why you at times feel closer to God when you are attending a church service, singing hymns

[116]

or praise songs? Could it be because that is where worship tends to take place? When you start praising Him, regardless of where you are, you will feel His presence, perhaps because you are no longer focused on yourself, but on Him. When we open the door to our hearts to love Him, He will meet us there.

4. Say His Name. People around you may be using God's name right and left (as a swear word in anger, or as a thoughtless expression). But the Bible states there is power in the name of Jesus because "Salvation is found in no one else, for there is no other name under heaven given to men by which we must be saved" (Acts 4:12). Say His name aloud - as the answer to all you seek, as the Source to calm your soul, as the One whose presence you long for and you will feel the power of His presence... and His peace.

5. Whisper a Prayer. There are times when we need Him but we just do not have a clue what to say or where to start. Begin by saying His name and then speak your heart's cry. For me, often times I just say "Jesus, I need you" or "Jesus, give me a heart for you." I believe the simplest of prayers are the ones that penetrate His heart - and ours - the quickest.

6. Go For a Walk. Exercise brings your body, mind and heart to life. Feel spiritually dead? Get outside in the open air, move around, confess to Him what is on your heart and let Him waken you up spiritually. My best times with God are when I am walking while I spill out my heart to Him.

7. Breathe Deeply. Sometimes we cannot feel God's presence because there is too much of everything else going on. Too much noise. Too much traffic. Too much confusion. Too many thoughts running uncontrolled in our minds. Too much anxiety. Center your mind on Him and start to breathe deeply. Try it out. Exhale all the distracting thoughts. Inhale a desire to feel His presence. Exhale your pre-occupation with self. Inhale a desire to know Him more intimately. Exhale all the worries of the moment. Inhale His peace. Now, don't you feel better already? Can you begin to feel that you are in His arms? There is a reason His Word says, "Be still and know that I am God" (Psalm 46:10).

Your Approach to Difficulties Will Determine Your Outcome!

Everyone confronts personal and professional difficulties. throughout life, whether the difficulties are physical, emotional, financial or based on race, class or gender. At times you are your own worst nightmare, when you let fear and self-doubt to stand in the way of success.

Difficulties are similar to mountains or giants; they will not move themselves. You have to climb the mountain or go around it, diminish it to a molehill with the power of the Word of God, or hollow out a tunnel straight through it. You must take action to overcome it, not sit at the foot of the mountain unresponsively hoping it will suddenly go away so you can be on your way.

Difficulties are more than just gigantic problems; problems occur whereas difficulties are there. Difficulties may have always been there, or they may pop up. A problem is more limited than a difficulty. Seldom does a problem last endlessly. You look for ways to solve problems to accomplish the best possible outcome; but, even if you take no action, a problem will reach some resolve eventually, though it may not be the outcome you would like. But a difficulty will not change itself or go away unless you do something about it.

There is no one who has a magic formula to deal with difficulties, but you can choose and implement some good practices when you are faced with difficulties that can help reduce an intimidating mountain into stepping stones to success.

First, You must believe in yourself, based on God's Word. Create in your mind a mental picture of yourself succeeding. Hold this picture persistently. Never allow it to fade. Your mind will look for ways to develop the picture. Do not build up difficulties in your imagination. The first step to conquering difficulties is to realize that the answer lies within you. Maturity and experience will give you the confidence that you can overcome any barrier.

Secondly, Seek help. Ask for council and support from a mentor, friend, or group. You do not have to deal with any difficulties alone. You should be aware you have many resources to help overcome that difficulty, within and outside the Church. If you are a leader or member of a group, seek the help of appropriate experts in that group, or bring together everyone you can think of - people in your church, among your close friends, throughout your sphere of influence and form a sort of support group to overcome the difficulty together.

Thirdly, Be like Jesus. Remove the emotion from the situation as soon as possible and remain clear thinking. TD Jakes said, "If you run into a wall, don't turn around and give up. Surround yourself with people who are creative for tearing

[119]

down walls. They will figure out how to climb it, or work around it." Use your clear thinking mind to figure out what you are up against. When difficulty initially hit, it may seem larger than life, but if you can step back and look at it realistically, often the solution becomes obvious to you. In this case you need to remove your emotion and set your team in motion to quickly and creatively strategize ways to cause the wall to tumble down.

Lastly, Break it down. When you know what you are dealing with, begin seeking ways to break it down. Have different people in your group pray on an individual bases as well corporately to solve the difficulty.

On the other side of the mountain, there is a saying which says, "The harder the test, the more glorious the triumph." What we obtain too cheaply, we esteem too lightly; This is what gives everything its value. During the thick of the battle to overcome a difficulty, you may not believe it, but the more difficulties you conquer, the easier the process becomes Your confidence in God will be perpetuating, and you may come to believe you can conquer a whole range of mountains through Christ who is strengthening you. Mark 11:23 says, "For verily I say to you, That whosoever shall say to this mountain, Be thou moved, and be thou cast into the sea; and shall not doubt in his heart, but shall believe that those things which he says shall come to pass; he shall have whatsoever he says."

Keep Moving Forward; Go Deeper

What is a mountain the life of a believer? The mountain is the issue in your life. The mountain is anything that is unfavorable on contradictory to the Word of God for

[120]

your life. A mountain is anything that is a roadblock to you completing God's will. A mountain is anything that is slowing down or stopping your progress in the kingdom of God.

Many believers spend time praying to God about their mountain. They describe the mountain in full detail to God. They tell God of the exact dimensions of the mountain. They cry and groan to God about what a hindrance or impossibility the mountain has become in their life.

Some believers even use the mountain as an excuse not to participate in their Christian life. Some believers make up doctrines and traditions about God to support why the mountain has remained in their life.

Many believers will pray to God for Him to speak to their mountain. God will never do what he has asked you to do. You pray to God to receive what Jesus has made available to you (Mark 11:24). It is your responsibility to speak to the mountain in your life.

Praying and fasting will not move a mountain. Prayer and fasting deal with unbelief or lack of confidence in God's Word (Matthew 17:20, Mark 9:28-29).

Many believers get into natural unbelief by what they see, hear, touch, smell, taste or feel. You must not let natural unbelief to be a contrary weight to your faith . Your spirit man must not be ruled by your un-generated, fallen flesh (Romans 5:5-8, Galatians 5:16). You must sow to the Spirit and reap life (Galatians 6:7).

Prayer is about your relationship with God through Jesus Christ. Prayer will increase your confidence about your

[121]

relationship with God. Prayer is how you receive from God (Matthews 7:8, Matthews 21:22).

Fasting food does not move God, it moves you. Fasting food takes you out of the natural realm and helps you to be sensitive to the spiritual realm of God. Fasting forces your flesh to submit to your spirit man. God becomes your total source. You live by the Word of God alone (Matthews 4:3-). Fasting teaches or disciplines your body to listen to your spirit man. You tell your body to line up with the Word of God and it obeys you. Your spirit man controls your body. Prayer does the same thing. Prayer disciplines your flesh to submit to your spirit man. You pray to God who you cannot see, hear, taste, smell and touch (Matthews 6:9). Prayer train your flesh to submit to your spirit man. Prayer and fasting are spiritual disciplines.

Prayer and fasting will shift you into a more confident position to speak to the mountain (Matthews 21:21).

Jesus never told us to pray to the Father about our mountain. He said for us to speak directly to the mountain; speak to the mountain in His name. In addition, Jesus never told us to ignore or deny the mountain. We are not to say, "I do not have a mountain" or "what problem?" We are not to practice positive thinking and say over and over; "I can climb over that mountain, I will go around that mountain, it will not stop me." A positive attitude is a good thing. But a positive attitude is not what Jesus said to do with mountains. Jesus said to speak to the mountain and tell it to be moved. (Mark 11:23).

Jesus says, "if you have faith as a mustard seed, you will say to this mountain, move from here to there, and it will move; and nothing will be impossible for you" (Matthews 17:20). A believer can say to the mountain be moved to some other dimension that I do not inhabit.

Authority is shown by speaking. You speak to individuals or things that you have the authority over. You do not ask; you direct and require. You show faith when you speak to things instead of asking God to speak for you. When you speak instead of asking, you demonstrate an understanding of God's Word. You cannot walk with God unless you agree with His Word (Amos 3:3). Faith involves you placing confidence in God's spoken word and responding to it. The God-like faith will illustrate itself by speaking and trusting God's Word. You will exhibit an understanding of God's divine order, will, and authority when you place trust in God's spoken word and respond.

Endurance Is The Key

I have been a Christian for many years, and as I look back on my life, I realize God has allowed one storm after another to pass through my life--a heartache, trial, burden, or tribulation after another. Each time, He has spoken to my heart, but I have never heard Him say, "Do not worry about anything. Just relax."

Instead, He often says, "Trust Me." There is something about hearing God speak these two words that cause a sense of peace to my heart. I may feel troubled over a decision and wonder what will happen next. However, when I sense God saying, "Trust Me," I stop thinking about all that could or could not go wrong and begin to rest in His presence and care. In addition, I also find that when I let go of my need to work something out, He handles all the details of my circumstances perfectly. Later in his life, David faced a very difficult set of circumstances. His life was being threatened again. Yet we find that he placed his hope in God and not in his own ability as King. In Psalm 55:22, we discover the key to his confidence. He writes, "Cast your burden upon the Lord and He will sustain you; He will never allow the righteous to be shaken." The word cast means to "toss over on God." In other words, David is telling us to toss the burdens of our hearts onto the Lord. After all, He is the only One who has power, the insight, and the ability to handle each one.

The Apostle Peter replicates David's words. He writes, "Cast all your anxiety on him (Christ) because he cares for you" (1 Peter 5:7). Only here, he tells us to roll our feelings of anxiety, fear, and discouragement over onto Christ our Savior, knowing He will raise us up and give us the guidance we need to face every threat. Therefore, when all hope seems to be gone and when sorrow or sin has clouded your way, ask God to reveal Himself to you, and tell Him that you want His will for your life and that you are asking Him to forgive you if you have knowingly disobeyed Him.

Chapter Fifteen: Let God Be Your Vindicator

After writing yesterday's journal, I was reminded of a sermon by TD Jakes. I loved to listen to it every chance I got during a time when I was really struggling with that whole "love your enemy" thing. He said we should be allowing God to be our vindicator, because when we try to vindicate ourselves (although we are right), we end up with such a disappointing feeling inside.

I had been struggling with an issue for years, but I had always managed to overlook things and keep the peace. Then one day, out of the blue, I snapped and let this person have it. By most people's criterion, I was perfectly within my right. However, by God's criterion, I knew immediately that I have just taken a giant leap. That disappointing feeling was forming in the bottom of my stomach.

Psalm 135:14 says, "For the Lord will vindicate his people and have compassion on his servants." Through my blundering, I learned how important it was to let God go to bat for me. It is not easy, because we tend to want the people who offended us to know that they are not going to get away with

[125]

treating us in that way. But by stepping in and taking matters into our own hands, what we are really implying is, "God, I don't fully trust you to take care of this, so I am going to do it my way." Setting out to vindicate myself put me on a spiritual slump that shook my foundation for months. It was a hard lesson to learn, but one that has made a fixed mark on my brain.

TD Jakes helped me to see that it is not my place to judge and sentence people. James 4:12 says there is only one Lawgiver and Judge, and I am pretty sure he was not talking about me. He went on to talk about the evidence of true character being this: treating people well who do not deserve it. It is hard. However, There have been people in my life who have treated me well when I didn't deserve it. I remember this when I get into circumstances where I feel hurt and want to even the score. I have learned to hand it over to God and accept that He will take care of it in His perfect way and time.

Dying to Self Daily

If you want God to make your enemy your footstool, you have to be still and know that He is God. When you are living upset and trying to force things to happen, God is going to step back and let you do it on your own. It takes faith to say, "God I know you are fighting my battles and will make my wrongs right. You promised it would work out for my good and I'm going to keep my joy and stay in peace." When you put your feet up and rest, God will take what was meant for evil and use it to your advantage. Your job is not to straighten people out; your job is to stay in peace. When you are in peace, God is fighting your battles. When you are at rest, God will make all your enemies your footstool.

[126]

God can vindicate you better than you can vindicate yourself. If you allow God to do it His way, it will be bigger, sweeter and more awarding; God can take the very people that are trying to push you down and use them to promote you.

God is a God of justice. He does not overlook what you are owed. You may let it go, but God does not let it go; He is going to make sure you get exactly what you deserve. Psalm 23:5 says, "You prepare a table before me in the presence of my enemies." God will bless you in front of your enemies. God can promote you anywhere, but He will give you recognition, favor, honor in front of the people who tried to pull you down.

All these things that come against us to try to get us upset, people talking, gossip, spreading rumors, those are all distractions. That is the enemy trying to get us off course, get us bent out of shape, waste valuable time and energy on something that does not really matter. Do not give that the time of day; that is not a battle you are suppose to fight. Stay on the path and God will bring it under your feet. He will make these enemies your footstool.

When you are in peace, it is a position of authority. When you are at rest, God is fighting your battles.

God knows how to apply tension, how to make somebody uncomfortable; you do not have to fight the battle. Stay on the path to your destiny and watch God make your enemies your footstool.

God says the issue may form, but you can stay in peace knowing that it is not going to prosper against you. All the

[127]

forces of darkness cannot keep you from your purpose and destiny.

God is saying, "I will fight your battles, but you got to give them to me; come back to that place of peace." Do not let people, problems get you upset. Let God be your vindicator. He knows how to make your wrongs right. If you will see these hindrances as being under your feet, God promises He will make your enemies your footstool. Instead of being a stumbling block, it will be a stepping stone. Nothing will keep you from your destiny and you will become everything God created you to be.

The Battle is the Lord's

This is to remind you the battle you are facing is not yours, but God's. If you are one of the children of God's, you can be certain that Satan will "roar and explode against you."

In Chronicles 20, a great crowd came against God's people. King Jehoshaphat and his people set their hearts to seek the Lord and fast. The king cried out to God a prayer that most of us have prayed at times during our spiritual journey. "We have no might against these that come against us, neither do we know what to do; but our eyes are upon you" (20:12). "The Spirit of God came in the midst of the congregation... saying, Be not afraid nor dismayed... for the battle is not yours, but God's" (20:14-15).

Isaiah gave this warning to all satanic forces: "Who have you reproached and blasphemed? And against whom have you exalted your voice?... Even against the Holy One of Israel" (Isaiah 37:23).

[128]

God informed his people Israel, and He informs us today: "The battle is not against you. It is Satan's rage against me, the Lord who abides in you." God said to Satan, "I know where you abide, and where you come and go, and your rage against me" (37:28).

Where is your battle? In your marriage? Your business or job? Your finances? Your health? Does your battle get more intense day after day? If you have a heart for Jesus and a desire to cling to Him, you will face the rage of hell. Yet that is still not your battle.

You can end this battle quickly if you decide simply by quitting and giving in to your fears and doubts. Satan will not bother those who give up their confidence in the Lord.

True, the battle is the Lord's, but we have a part, and that is to trust and believe his promises in the face of hopelessness and what seem to be impossibilities. "Why say thou, O Jacob, and speak, O Israel, My way is hid from the Lord, and my judgment is passed over from my God?" (Isaiah 40:27).

Faith demands that I turn over all my problems, all my critical circumstances, all my fears, all my anxieties, into the hands of the Lord. When I have done all I can do, and I know my battle is beyond my power, I must submit all into His hands.

Our Lord Jesus Christ knows the raging of Satan, and we must truly believe He will act on our behalf. He will bring us through floods and fires and put to chase all spiritual enemies. Here is God's Word concerning what He will do: "Because of your rage against me..., it has come into my ears,

[129]

therefore I will put a hook in your nose, and my bridle in your lips, and I will turn you back by the way you came" (Isaiah 37:29).

If you will hold fast to your faith, trusting Him, resting in His promises, rejecting all lies of Satan coming into your mind, then expect God to come by his Spirit into your situation and bring an expected end to your particular battle. He will move heaven and earth to deliver you and make a way. The way out is to trust, trust, trust. "He makes wars to cease" (Psalm 46:19).

Chapter Sixteen:
How to Heal Emotions

Emotion can plunge you like an empty brown bag. The mind can lure you in circles of confusion and physical hurt. Emotion and mind equals blocks and binds. The quality of your life is an image of the quality of your own inner feelings. I am going to share with you how to heal your emotion in a few simple steps, if you want to be made whole. This is only for those that would actually like to heal their emotion and develop a better quality of life.

Before you can heal emotion, you must understand what emotion really is. "Emotion is a response to a differing to the inflexible opinions of the mind." Nothing more.

Emotion is a response. Emotional pain is nothing more than an inner contradiction. It is the differing between what you want to experience and what you actually experience. You must accept contradiction as being a natural part of the human experience. When you let go of your inflexible intellectual opinions as to how you think things should be, what is there to contradict? Nothing. No conflict. No pain. All you need to do is discipline yourself to not to respond to things and drop your inflexible intellectual opinions, and you cannot even experience negative human emotions at all. And that is the absolute truth.

Anger is a Response to Loss. To heal anger, all you really need to do is examine what you lost and then either get it back or let it go. Usually letting it go is the best answer. Most anger is rooted in the loss of the control of things. Drop your need to control everything, and you drop your anger with everything.

Anxiety is a Response to Uncertainty. Nothing is certain in life. Accept uncertainty. Most anxiety is the expectation of facing something that you do not know the outcome to. So what? Drop your opinion about needing to know, and you drop anxiety. Drop anxiety, and you are given confidence.

Boredom is a Response to Laziness. The only way to heal boredom is to do something you have not done before. Boredom is nothing more than a lack of interest in what you are doing. You need to find interesting things to do in this life. You need to make things interesting in this life. Be creative. If you are experiencing boredom, then perhaps you are boring.

Depression is a Response to Failure. Depression is the inability to face extrinsic circumstances. You must accept the circumstances in your life, before you have the strength to change the circumstances of your life. You need to accept your failures as being learning experiences. Failure is a dysfunction, circumstances that are not working out. Depression is response to circumstances in your life that also are not working out for you, draining all your energy. Accept the situation. Man up. Change your situation. Move forward.

Desire is a Response to Lack. Desire is to wish and to want. There is no controlling force in it. The sense of lack develop the lack. Emotional leaning pushes things away. The moment you drop your desire, is the very moment that you are granted the strength to do. Action makes happen. Not desire.

Fear is a Response to Change. All fear is rooted in the fear of death, the fear of change. You must accept death as being a natural part of life in the human experience. You must accept change as being the natural way of things. Fear can also come because of dehydration. Drink plenty of filtered water. The moment you accept change as being natural, is the moment you truly start to live again. It is called a life without fear.

Frustration is a Response to Expectation. Frustration comes from trying too hard to force things into a deadline. Heaven on earth takes time. The only thing that neutralizes frustration, is patience. The moment you let go expectancy, and simply focus on what you are doing with clearness and concentration, is the very moment that you are actually granted the ability to function with proficiency, and time slows down.

Hate is a Response to Prejudice. Prejudice is predetermined dislike and hostility based on absolutely on no real reason or direct experience of things. What are inflexible intellectual opinions that are based on no direct experience, understanding, or wisdom called? Ignorance. You heal hate by sowing warmth, wisdom and understanding, and that comes from experiencing things directly for yourself. And if you do not like what you experience, fine, but you just might discover there is more to love in this world than you think.

Resentment is a Response to Feeling Treated Unfairly. Nothing is fair in this life. If nothing is fair in this life, then everything is fair in this life. The world is full of people that want things handed to them, for nothing. You deserve nothing

[133]

more than whatever you have the strength to produce in this world.

The moment you realize that emotion is nothing more than a response to the inflexible intellectual opinions of the ego, is the very moment that you can actually heal the emotion. It is simply a matter of identifying the emotion, accepting disagreement and dropping inflexible intellectual opinions. This prescription works for any emotion you experience. It does not matter what you have experienced. The process of healing is the same, regardless of the outer limit that one experiences.

The difficulty with this little equation is not the equation. The equation works. The difficulty is that people think their emotions are real feelings. They are not. Emotions are only responses that effect their true feelings. True feelings are resounding sensations. The difficulty is that people go, around and around in circles within their own minds, trapped in their inflexible intellectual opinions. People must process things, but the entire point of processing is to stop processing to achieve an end to reach acceptance.

Chapter Seventeen:
The Kingdom of God

"But rather seek ye first the Kingdom of God, and all these things shall be added unto you ' Luke 12:31.

In life we are indoctrinated to prepare ourselves economically, socially, and academically; these are the most powerful areas of the human social experience. Those who are the most educated have a tendency to make the most money, and those who make the money are more socially exposed, and those who are more socially exposed gain entry to all three of the above areas victoriously. This is true in the System of this World, but it is not at all true of the Kingdom of God. The Kingdom of God includes total power. To the extent, that the power it has affected every area of our lives. It has nothing to do with our level of education, or social positioning, or how much money we make, but how surrendered we are to that Kingdom. When we think about a Kingdom, you think about the area or region of a king; a sort of territory of a Sovereign ruler. Well, Jesus tells us in the gospel of Luke Chapter 12, to seek first the Kingdom. He informs us that the Kingdom of God has supremacy. It is the main goal, it is the first preference. Why does Jesus instruct us to seek it first? He is revealing the Power of The Kingdom. He is allowing us to know that all that we want and would seek after is present and active in the Kingdom. It has everything we need, because it is the territory of the One who is everything that we could ever need.

There is no lack in the Kingdom, there is no sickness in the Kingdom, and there is no want of success in the Kingdom. The dilemma that we have as Christians is that we seek everything else but the Kingdom. Why? The answer is very obvious. We do not really know and believe the Power of The Kingdom of God. One reason we do not know the Power of The Kingdom is because we do not know what the Kingdom of God is. I will explain it: The Kingdom of God is most easily explain as the expression of God's leadership. It comes from the Greek word "basileia" and it means royal power or dominion. So the Kingdom of God is the demonstration of God's rule and power. It is not just a place but it is a system of sovereign government and authority. This is the point that Jesus declared: that the Kingdom has come, repent. God's government was demonstrated at the revealing of Jesus Christ as the Messiah (Promised King).

This Kingdom is not a natural Kingdom but a spiritual kingdom. The Kingdom of God is so powerful that it replaces anything other than itself. This is why the Word of God instruct us to seek it first, because in it is everything else we need. The Kingdom of God is a kingdom of provision, healing, restoration, and deliverance. There is nothing in your life that the Kingdom of God cannot take care of. As we seek the Kingdom of God; all of the fullness of the Kingdom will be seen in our lives.

If you invited the president of the richest country per capita in the world to your birthday celebration and you ran out of food, would you worry? No. Why? Because everything

[136]

that you would ever need to supply for that event is in his possession. Clearly, we will acknowledge the natural provision of human beings but overlook the Power and Provision of the wealthiest one ever: Jehovah Jireh our provider. The Power of the Kingdom of God is the revelation that He is more than enough in every circumstance that I face in my life. It is the realization that we are His children and He is our Father and He is the King of Kings and has all power. Jesus has invited us into this government and has given us the Keys to this Kingdom, that whatever we bind on earth shall be bound in heaven, and whatever we loose on earth shall be loosed in heaven.

This Kingdom is the most powerful Kingdom in existence, because it is the place where God's sovereign Authority is acknowledged in the earth. We have entry to all of the resources that are active in heaven, right here on earth. Faith in the Word of God is the key that releases the power of the Kingdom of God in the various situations of life. As we seek this government, this way of thinking, this dominion we are setting ourselves up to receive the blessings that are present in that Kingdom. Are you walking in the reality of the Power of the Kingdom of God in your Life? It already belongs to you through the finish work of Christ!

The requirements of God for the believer

Once you become a part of God's family, the enemy's aim is to make your life miserable. Because he knows he no longer has rule over your soul or eternal destiny, these are totally in God's care, his focus changes. He moves immediately, wishing to cause headache, frustration, and disappointment within your life. He will halt at nothing to accomplish this miserable goal. Why? He longs for you to become so grief-stricken, enraged and filled with tension that you grow weary and forsake your faith. However, this is never a choice for a true believer.

We are chosen by God to be conquerors through our Lord Jesus Christ (Romans 8:37). Paul writes, "I am convinced that neither death, nor life, nor angels, nor principalities, nor things present, nor things to come, nor powers, nor height, nor depth, nor any other created thing, will be able to separate us from the love of God, which is in Christ Jesus our Lord" (Romans 8:38-39). As I have explained, God has an explanation for the dilemmas we face. However, He also has ways to handle each one. When life takes a sudden turn in a dark direction, we have to make a decision to trust and obey God's instructions, or to struggle with our fears and uncertainties on our own. It is God's wish that we will turn to Him in prayer for wisdom and strength.

Learn to respond correctly

In 2 Chronicles, after a series of errors, King Jehoshaphat realized himself and the nation of Judah in a very bad situation. In fact, the danger facing them was fatal. And for a time, it seemed Judah would be defeated. The king had attempted to mend fences with his enemies, something he should not have done because this only created more trouble. Instead of calming enemy forces, the threatening armies plotted a plan to march on Jerusalem and destroy it. When king Jehoshaphat received the message of the impending danger, fear filled his heart. However, instead of letting fear to control and rule his emotions, he did the one things he knew would bring hope to a deteriorating situation: he turned to the Lord in prayer. In other words, fear was not his final decision. It came as a quick response to his circumstances, but he refused to cling to it. Instead, he responded in faith through prayer. When a storm strikes without warning, what is your first response?

Many of us have had the same kind of experience. Suddenly, our lives take on a dark and stormy turn. Our minds floods instantly with thoughts of terror, but God's Spirit also mounts up within us to remind us that He is in control of even the most messy situation. If you forget everything, remember this: God is always in control. Nothing that comes to you catches Him by surprise. He is Lord over every feature of life and for sure over every storm, no matter how deep or dark it becomes.

Jehoshaphat received information that his enemies were planning against him. He was a just king, the king of Judah for almost twenty-five years. He decided to bring about a revival of faith among God's people. It is believed that he had an army that consisted of nearly a million men. However, that number appeared very small when compared to the armies of his enemies, the Moabites and the Ammonites. When their plot started to unfold, instantly panic swept over his heart and the hearts of the people. Quickly, he cast down his wrong thoughts by turning to God in prayer: "Then some came and reported to Jehoshaphat saying, 'A great multitude is coming against you from beyond the sea, out of Aram and behold, they are in Hazazon-tamar (that is Engedi).' Jehoshaphat was scared and turned his attention to seek the Lord, and declared a fast throughout all Judah" (2 Chronicles 20:2-3).

[139]

Suddenly, the king knew there was only one place to grasp hope, and that was in God's sovereign protection. He remembered what the Lord had done for Israel in the past and knew that God would not forsake the nation now.

"So Judah gathered together to seek help from the Lord; they even came from all the cities of Judah to seek the Lord. So Jehoshaphat stood in the assembly of Judah and Jerusalem, in the house of the Lord before the new court, and he said, "O Lord, the God of our fathers, are You not God in the heavens? And are You not ruler over all the kingdoms of the nations? Power and might are in Your hand so that no one can stand against You" (2 Chronicles 20:4-6). Devotional prayers are prayers that we communicate to gain a more greater sense of God's presence surrounding us. Every morning, before we get out of bed, we need to ask God to order our steps, to help us to be aware of His nearness and the many ways He seeks to direct us. Later, before we head out, we need to make time to be alone with Him in prayer, study, and worship.

Be aware that the first thing Judah did was to gather in God's presence. The people desired to be near Him, and they also desired Him to know that they needed Him. Their prayer was not devotional; it was a cry for help. However, before they came to this fork in the road, they had established a relationship with the Lord. This means that their devotion was set on God. Jehoshaphat had labored to develop an environment of worship to God and none other. Many times, God will let us face a situation that is far too great for us to handle on our own. We need Him, and this is , without question, where Judah was standing, in a place of extreme need and dependence on Him.

The Importance of prayer

The next move they took was to change their thinking. As long as you believe God will not answer your prayers, He most likely will not, but not because He is not willing. Sometimes, we move out before Him. We might pray and then jump up and think we need to fix the situation. We do not give God a chance, and we truly do not give Him time to answer our prayers. Waiting on God is important to seeing how He will move on our behalf. At times, He will answer immediately, as we shall see by examining this chapter further. Other times, He tells us to wait until He has all the building blocks in place to achieve what He desires to do. You could be tangling with a dilemma that has lingered for weeks, months, and even years. You might wonder if God really knows what you are going through or if He cares. Waiting is not passive. It is an active move of faith. A individual chooses to wait on God because he or she wants God's best.

When we face challenges in life but we do not think correctly about God, then any prayer we say will be in vain. You have heard individuals say, "I have told God about my problem, but nothing has happened. I have constantly prayed and He has not given me a solution. In fact, I feel worse off. Why doesn't God answer my prayer? Why is He so silent, especially when He knows that I am heartbroken and the problem is expanding larger each day?"

Jehoshaphat not only prayed, he started to remember all that God had done for the people. "Did You not, O our God,

[141]

drive out the inhabitants of this land before Your people Israel and give it to the descendants of Abraham Your Friend forever?" (Chronicles 20:7). The king desired to make sure that God remembered that He was the One who brought His people to this point. He had covered them, and now they were facing a horrendous nightmare, one that could undo all that the Lord had done. There will be times in your life when you will face situations at work or in service at your church when you will feel as though all that you have gained on an assignment could be lost as a result of another's selfish behaviors. Judah's enemies desired to dominate and take over them because they worshiped the true and living God. It is very simple. Some may dispute that there was material spoil to be gained, but what was really at risk was God's ability to provide and protect those He loved.

Right believing, right thinking

Right believing and right thinking always produce right results. Therefore, if you will follow the next few moves, I promise you that God will deal with the dilemma that you are facing. He will provide an answer. But first, the question you must answer is, am I willing to abide by God's answer, regardless of what that answer entails? If you come to God in prayer with a preconceived idea of what the answer needs to look like, then you will be saddened. There may be times when God motivates you to pray a certain way. This is certainly obvious in the prayer that Jehoshaphat prayed. God motivated him to remember the ways He had worked in the past to develop an atmosphere of hope and courage among the people.

Why would you pray the following and expect God to act: "Lord, I do not know how You will help me. I feel very weak and hopeless. I cannot feel Your affection. Have You left me? God stands right beside you as you pray. He has never failed you, and He never will. If you decide not to trust Him, you will encounter times of failure and defeat. However, if you will trust in Him, believe Him no matter how deep the valley becomes, He will raise you up and bring you safely through the trial. There are numerous things we need to learn to pray with faith and power.

God is concerned about your problem. Jehoshaphat prayed, "Lord, the God of our fathers, are You not God in the heavens? ...Are you not ruler over all the kingdoms of the nation?" (2 Chronicles 20:6). He was recalling to himself and those who heard his prayer that there was no one as great and as faithful as the Lord God. The people remembered God had led them out of Egypt and brought them to this point. But their minds needed to be renewed, refocused, on the Lord. They could not move another step without Him because He was ruler of all things. There are times when we need to take this same step. The answer to our prayers may appear obvious. The solution to our problems can only be solved one way, and that is God's way. However, emotions such as doubt, fear, unbelief, and even deep sadness can darken our faith and diminish our trust in Him.

God has made a promise to you. The moment you pray and ask Him to come into your life and save you from your sins, He does just that. He saves you from eternal

[143]

damnation and set up an eternal covenant with you that can never be broken. Your personal relationship with Christ begins the moment you accept what He did for you on Calvary's cross as payment for your transgressions. Three days later, He rose and ascended to the Father's right hand, where He makes nonstop intercession on your behalf (Hebrew 7:25). Whatever need you have, Jesus is committed to asking the Father to provide it for you.

Picture the God of the universe, who is not only aware of your needs but yearns to meet each one and give you the desires of your heart. Through salvation, you become a member of the family of God. As His son or daughter, this relationship is unchangeable. Your joys, problems and heartaches also belong to God. The same was true for the nation of Judah. God was with them. Actually, He was the Chief over all that took place the day they marched into battle.

Next, you need to remember is something we have stated earlier. **No problem is too great for Him to handle.** He is bigger than any sorrow or disappointment you will ever confront. You may be having a hard time at work. Your boss is pressing you to perform with tremendous speed and accuracy in a much shorter time. The stress is horrendous, and you know that you cannot walk out because you have monthly bills to pay.

There are times when He lets a situation to get out of order to show us He is over all things. If the armies mounting an attack against Jehoshaphat had gathered but then became afraid and disbanded, more than likely the people of Judah would have become proud. They would have celebrated instead of turning to the Lord in prayer. Whatever drives you to God is good for you. This is because it reveals your weaknesses, your inability to handle life without Him, and your need for Him. Confronted with a very serious physical dilemma, the apostle Paul writes,

Concerning this I implore the Lord three times that it might leave me. And He has said to me,

"My grace is sufficient for you, for power is perfected in weakness." Most gladly, therefore, I
will rather boast about my weaknesses, so that the power of Christ may dwell in me.

Therefore I am well content with weaknesses, with insults, with distresses, with persecutions, with difficulties, for Christ's sake; for when I am weak, then I am strong. (2 Corinthian 12:8-10)

The connection of Paul's words is this: "When I am weak, emotionally, physically, and spiritually, then I am made strong through faith in Jesus Christ." Strength does not come through human ability to solve hard issues; it comes through personal surrender, first to Him and then to the predicament. He has permitted to come into your life. In order to gain the victory, you must permit Him to take control of all that concerns you. When you do, He will rejuvenate you and provide the energy, strength, and wisdom you need for every situation.

Never ignore God's leading to pray. Many say they are too busy to stop and pray. Others seem afraid of what He may reveal to them if they do. They pause because they want to maintain control over their lives. This does not make sense. Picture trying to withhold something from the God of the

[145]

universe, the One who knows all things, has created all things, and is over all things. All that sustains us in times of sin and resistance is the grace that He has extended to us. It is His grace that permits us to have free will that is limited. In other words, God will let us go so far, but if we do not respond to His counsel, we will reap the consequences of our sinful behavior. He tells us in Numbers, "Be sure your sin will find you out" (32:23). Sin involves many decisions and behaviors. In every case, it leads to open rebellion against God.

Often the dilemmas we confront are the result of our decision to say no to God. He gave Adam and Eve a very straight-forward command: "Don't eat the fruit of the tree in the center of the garden" (Genesis 2:16-17). Yet they didn't take Him seriously. They clearly understood His command, yet they chose to disobey Him. Actually, they did not understand the consequences of their sin would be. But God knew, and this is why we should obey Him, on the basis of who is doing the talking. If He says no or wait, we need to remember He knows much more than we know. He may be saving us from deep heartache. Or He could be in the process of preparing a great blessing for us to enjoy. If we rush ahead, we could end up in deep trouble or missing the very thing that will open a door of personal joy and satisfaction.

Another point you need to remember is this: **you do not have to understand how God will handle your problems.** He knows exactly what needs to be done. Your job is to set the focus of your heart on obeying Him. This includes seeking Him during prayer. If you are going to find an answer for your problems, you need to make this a top priority. Often the reason we do not receive solutions to our prayers is because we are in a hurry. We are not willing to wait on God's answer.

One of the most rewarding experiences you will have is watching God work because you waited for His timing.

Timing is extremely important to God. He has a major destiny planned for our lives and for the events of history. He knows when a small sparrow falls to the ground, and He knows when you need to make a move in a certain direction. The key to learning this principle is to be willing to wait for His timing, for His leading, and for His guidance. As you wait, set a goal to be in prayer. You can whisper a prayer within your heart all day long, a week or even much longer. "God, heal my child." "Save this person on my job who does not know You." "Show me the direction I need to go from this point forward." "Give me a promise to hold and to cling to when I feel alone." "Protect me." "Keep me focused on You so that I might know Your truth and hold it within my heart." There are numerous prayers that you can pray in an instant while you spend time in quiet devotion with Him. The king of Judah "turned his attention to seek the Lord" (2 Chronicles 20:3). He did not seek his commanding generals together. Instead, he went to the Lord in prayer, and God heard him. In fact, the Lord saw and heard the prayers of His people. Prayer should be a natural protocol to any trouble you face.

The power of dependency

There are seasons when God will not let you to solve an issue by yourself. He sends an opponent or enemy, and He waits to see if you will cry out to Him. Although they had a large army, Judah was aware they could not win the battle. It was obvious that they would lose. There will be seasons in our lives when we will know the same thing, that there is no way to win the attack apart from God's help. The truth of the matter, God is never perplexed by your dilemmas. Actually, He had the solution in His mind while you were in your mother's womb and even before you knew there was an issue.

One of the greatest valuable resource you can have as a believer is a group of godly friends who love the Lord and are committed to living their lives for Him. Actually, you need at least one person who loves you no matter what and accepts you, just as you are. God is this kind of friend to us, but He also wishes for us to have friends whom we can turn to at periods for confirmation and instruction.

There will be seasons when God uses a friend to come to your aid to help you solve the dilemma you are facing. Pride dictates to us that we do not need anyone else. We can be there for others, but we desire to take care of personal matters without the help of anyone else. However, we cannot handle it alone, we need one another. We need honest feedback sometimes, and we also need to know others are cheering for our achievement. When you choose your closest friends, select people who only want to grow in their walk with the Lord and are committed to living godly lives. When you do, you will notice that life is a lot smoother. Far too often, we cling close to people who have the ability to pull us down spiritually. Over the journey of life, we will know all types of people. I am referring to the ones who make up your inner circle of friends. choose wisely, and you will notice that you will be blessed beyond anything you can conceive by their friendship. Once you learn how to lean on Him, God will usually allow you to be a part of the answer. But first, we must:

[148]

focus,
wait,
listen, and
obey.

Jehoshaphat and the people of Judah grew very determined in their faith. There are seasons when you will need to be still before God, seasons when the only thing you can do is trust Him, even though the circumstance may appear as though it is spinning entirely out of control. The king maintained his prayer, "Should evil come upon us, the sword, or judgment, or pestilence, or famine, we will stand before this house and before You (for Your name is in this house) and cry to You in our distress, and You will hear and deliver us" (2 Chronicles 20:9). The whole nation had gathered before the Lord, husband and wives along with their children (v. 13). No one stayed home. The threat and the hazard were too great to ignore.

"Then in the middle of the assembly the Spirit of the Lord came on Jahaziel the son of Zechariah... and he said, "Listen, all Judah and the inhabitants of Jerusalem and king Jehoshaphat: thus says the Lord to you, 'Do not fear or be dismay because of this great multitude, for the battle is not yours but God's" (vv. 14-15). We should desire to shout, "Praise God," at the sight of these words. The Lord was about to show up on the scene to show Himself strong.

When you truly seek Him, God will make you responsive to His will. When He speaks to your heart, you will know it is His voice. Jesus stresses this point. According to the book of John, He says, "My sheep hear My voice, and I know them, and they follow Me" (10:27). You might think,

[149]

God never speaks to me. He speaks to those who have accepted Him as Savior, who have made Him Lord of their lives, and who take the time to listen. By listening, I am referring to being willing to be still before Him in prayer, still in your heart, mind, and spirit.

Prayer is a move of faith, not a pathway to nervousness. He calms our fears during His presence. We need what Jehoshaphat did and that was to transfer his total dependence on God. I don't know the dilemma you are facing, but if you will write this down someplace where you can see it, God will direct your eyes back to these words: "Do not fear or be dismayed because of this great multitude, for the battle is not yours but God's." This is the secret to victory: God never loses. He might not act as fast as you desire Him to act, but He is always fully on time, never early or never late.

Chapter Eighteen:
It Is Finished

"I have finished the work which You have given Me to do"
John 17:4

The death of Jesus Christ is the fulfillment in history of the very mind and intent of God. There is no place for beholding Jesus as a martyr. His death was not something that just happened to Him, something that might have been prevented. His death was the very reason He came.

Never build your case for forgiveness on the thought that God is our Father and He will forgive us because He loves us. That denies the revealed truth of God in Jesus Christ. It makes the Cross unnecessary and the redemption was not all it was hyped up to be. God forgives sin only because of the death of Jesus. God could forgive people in no other way then by the death of His Son and Jesus is glorified and honored as Savior because of His death. We see Jesus..." (Hebrew 2:9). The greatest note or triumph ever sounded on the Cross of Christ, "It is finished" (John 19:30). That is the concluding words in the redemption of human beings.

Anything that diminishes or erase the holiness of God, through a false view of His love, denies the truth of God as revealed by Jesus Christ. Never let yourself believe that Jesus stands with us, and against His Father, out of pity and compassion, or that He became a curse for us out of sympathy for us. Jesus became a curse for us by divine order. Our part in understanding the enormous meaning of His curse is the conviction of sin. Conviction is given to us as a gift of shame and repentance; it is the huge mercy of God. Jesus loathes the sin in people, and Calvary is the extent of His hatred.

Jesus does not need your help

Jesus' words, "It is finished" appears only twice in the New Testament - John 19:28 and John 19:30.

"After this Jesus, knowing that all was now finished said, 'I thirst.' A jar full of sour wine stood there, so they put a sponge full of the sour wine on a hyssop branch and held it to his mouth. When Jesus had received the sour wine, he said, 'It is finished' and he bowed his head and gave up his spirit." (John 29:28-30).

"It is finished," which is one of Jesus' most significant statement, is translated from the single Greek word 'tetelestai.' The grammatical structure of the Greek word, perfect passive indicative, is very significant.

The perfect tense suggests the progress of an action has been completed and the result of that action is ongoing and with full effect. The passive voice suggests that the subject of the sentence is being acted upon, and the indicative mood suggests a statement of fact and an actual occurrence from the writer's or speaker's perspective. This information is again very significant to understanding the importance of Jesus' words. Let me explain.

What did Jesus finish?

Jesus tells us the answer throughout the gospels, and the New Testament writers tell us the answer throughout the epistles.

"Do not think that I have come to abolish the Law or the Prophets; I have not come to abolish them but to fulfill them" (Matthew 5:17).

Jesus obeyed the Father by being the perfect fulfillment of the Law of God and the prophesies regarding the Savior. Jesus finished the work given Him by His Father.

"Do not think that I have come to bring peace to the earth. I have not come to bring peace but a sword. For I have come o set a man against his father, and a daughter against her mother, and a daughter-in-law against her mother-in-law, and person's enemies will be those of his own household" (Matthew 10:34-36).

"Do you think that I have come to give peace on earth? No, I tell you, but rather division" (Luke 12:51).

Jesus did not come to preach a message of coexistence, tolerance, or ecumenism. Jesus made it clear that you are either with the one and only true God or against Him. Such truth was and is today the most divisive message the world has ever known. Jesus finished the work.

"I have come in my Father's name, and you do not receive me. If another comes in his own name, you will receive him" (John 5:43).

"For I have come down from heaven, not to do my own will but the will of him who sent me" (John 6:38).

Jesus came in the name of God and to perfectly do His will. Jesus finished the work.

"If I am not doing the works of my Father, then do not believe me, but if I do them, even though you do not believe me, believe the works, that you may know and understand the Father is in me and I am in the Father" (John 10:37-38).

Jesus came to perfectly do the works of His Father so people could understand that the Father is in me and I am in the Father (John 10:30). Jesus finished the work.

"I have come into the world as light, so that whoever believes in me may not remain in darkness. If anyone hears my words and does not keep them, I do not judge him; for I did not come to judge the world but to save the world. The one who rejects me and does not receive my words has a judge; the word that I have spoke will judge him on the last day" (John 12:46-48).

Jesus came as the light of the world, giving fallen mankind the opportunity to move from utter darkness into His marvelous light. He came to save people. Jesus finished the work given to Him. Jesus came as fully God and fully man to be the incarnation of the Truth of God.

"Since therefore the children share in flesh and blood, he himself likewise partook of the same things, that through death he might destroy the one who has the power of death that is , the devil, and deliver all those who through fear of death were subject to lifelong slavery. For surely it is not angels that he helps, but he helps the offspring of Abraham. Therefore he had

[154]

to be made like his brothers in every respect, so that he might become a merciful and faithful high priest in the service of God, to make propitiation for the sins of the people. For because he himself has suffered when tempted, he is able to help those who are being tempted" (Hebrew 2:14-18).

Jesus came to make reconciliation between God and man possible. Also, He came to die for and purify His Bride, the Church. Jesus came to glorify His Father through His life, death, and resurrection. Furthermore, Jesus came to make a way, the only way for people to find mercy, grace, and help in time of need.

Having explained the "it" (the work God had given His Son to achieve on earth, at the cross,) the great exchange took place. The eternal debt owed for the sin of mankind was paid in full. God looked upon His perfect, precious, and priceless Son as if He had lived the filthy, detestable, sin-stained lives of fallen mankind. And, for those who repent and receive Jesus as their Lord and Savior, God looks on them as if they had lived His Son's perfect, precious, and priceless life.

Chapter Nineteen: The Supernatural Power of Praise

There is a supernatural power that is released during praise that changes both the physical and non-physical realm. When the praises go up, the glory comes down. It is that easy. If we wish to see breakthrough in our personal lives, churches, cities, regions and nations, then we need to comprehend the supernatural power of praise.

Praise is defined as to commend, applaud or magnify. For the believer, praise to God is a statement of worship, lifting up and glorifying the Lord. It is a statement of humbling ourselves and centering our attention on the Lord with heart-felt expressions of love, adoration and thanksgiving. High praises bring our spirit into a high point of fellowship and intimacy between ourselves and God; it amplifies our awareness of our spiritual union with the Most High God. Praise carries us into the realm of the supernatural and into the power of God. "Blessed is the people that know the joyful sound: they shall walk, O Lord, in the light of thy countenance" (Psalm 89:15).

There are many actions involve with praise to God, verbal expressions of adoration and thanksgiving, singing, playing instruments, shouting, dancing, lifting or clapping our hands. Unpretending praise and worship pleases the Lord. According to Scripture, the various expressions of praise bring blessing to the Lord. He patiently awaits the fragrance of our affections, desiring to reveal His sweet presence and power in our midst. "The true worshipers shall worship the Father in spirit and in truth: for the Father seeks such to worship him" (John 4:23).

Praise is a lifestyle

All too often, praise to God is something that many people leave at church, an event that happens only when they come together with other Believers. However, praise should be a part of a Christian's lifestyle, combines as a part of their daily prayer-life, at work, in the car, at home in bed, or anywhere, praise to the Lord brings the refreshing of the Lord's presence, along with His power and anointing. "I will bless the Lord at all times: his praise shall continually be in my mouth" (Psalm 34:1).

Thank God for what you have left

I now fully understand that each day given to me is a blessing. Even on those days when I feel I have nothing to feel blessed about. I am alive, breath, laugh, play, walk, talk, smile. I have good and strong useful hands to carry things, to write words to share with others. To hold those I love and adore close to me tightly, to hug my children, grandchildren, family and friends.

[157]

I have aching feet some days and knees now starting to show signs of aging, but I am still able to stand alone, walk alone, run when the need present itself. I have a month to speak with a voice that can now be heard without fearing someone will silence me. I am blessed to have come out of a very dark season in my life when I felt ignored and abandoned by my family. I treasure the word blessing now in every sense of it. I take into account my blessings daily, hourly because I know those who are the blessings in my life today may be gone tomorrow. I treasure them all. I truly have many times in my life to have taken the blessings sent to me from God for granted but not today.

I hear so many people fighting with each other, marriages being less valued, friendships divided because of the words that people use on each other. In the crossfire of them all sit the innocent children who ends up being their escape goat. Instead of these people choosing to be happy with all they have, they focus on all the wrong things. Children are a blessing sent to us from God to treasure them, hold them, love them, and protect them. I never fully understood what it meant when someone would tell me to count my blessings and to be grateful for all I had. So now I get it 'count my blessing' are all the good, the bad, the ugly that goes with being human.

Walk in the Spirit

Believers have the Spirit of Christ within them, the hope of glory (Colossians 1:27). Those who walk in the Spirit will show forth daily, minute-by-minute holiness. This is brought about by consciously choosing by faith to depend on the Holy Spirit to guide in thought, word, and deed (Romans 6:11-14). Failure to rely on the Holy Spirit's guide will end in a believer not living up to the calling and standing that salvation provides (John 3:3; Ephesians 4:1). We can know that we are walking in the Spirit if our lives are showing forth the fruit of the Spirit which is love, joy, peace, patience, kindness, goodness, faithfulness, gentleness, and self-control (Galatians 5:22-23). Walking with the Spirit is the same as allowing the word of Christ (the Bible) to abundantly dwell in us (Colossians 3:16).

In the end there is thankfulness, singing and joy (Ephesians 5:18-20; Colossians 3:16). Born again believers of God will be led by the Spirit of God (Romans 8:14). When a Christian choose not to walk in the Spirit, thereby sinning and grieving Him, provision has been made for restoration through confession of the wrong doing (Ephesians 4:30; 1 John 1:9). To "walk in the Spirit" is to follow the Spirit's leading. It is basically essential to walk with the Spirit, allowing Him to guide your steps and conform your mind. To summarize, just as we have received Christ by faith, by faith He asks us to walk in Him until we are taken to heaven and will hear from the Father, "Well done" (Colossians 2:5; Matthew 25:23).

The most important question to ask ourselves is "Am I in Christ?" If the answer is yes, then, "There is therefore now no condemnation for those who are in Christ Jesus" (Romans 8:1).

The individual who is "in Christ Jesus" does not walk after the flesh, but after and in step with the Holy Spirit. He walks according to the guidance of the Spirit. To be "filled with the Spirit" is to be under the control of the Spirit. Every believer has the Holy Spirit. Our responsibility is to yield to Him. He has the spirit of life in Christ Jesus. The results of our justification through faith in Christ is a new creation, no longer under the control of the flesh, but in the spirit, a spiritual person.

God does not erase the flesh. It is still there striving and warring against the spirit, and it will be there until the Christian is taken up into heaven to be with God.

Apostle Paul tells us the individual who is "in Christ Jesus" devotes himself to the guidance and control of the Holy Spirit. He gives us encouragement, guidance, correction, and leads us in the paths of righteousness so that we become more like Christ.

Another question you should ask yourself is, "Am I walking according to the flesh? Or Am I walking in the Spirit? Our response determines what we produce in our daily lives. The apostle Paul said, "Do not walk according to the flesh, but according to the Spirit (Romans 8:4).

How do you recognize the difference? For those who are according to the flesh set their minds on the things of the flesh, but those who are according to the Spirit, the things of the Spirit (v. 5).

Is my life conduced under the control of the Spirit? If so, I will produce the fruit of the Spirit in my life (Galatians 5:22-23). It will be the opposite of the works of the flesh. (vv. 19-21).

How is your walk? Your walk is determined by your thinking. "As a man thinks in his heart, so is he." Set your mind on the things of the flesh, let it be dominated by fleshly thoughts, and you will produce the works of the flesh. Let your

[160]

mind be under the control of the Holy Spirit and you will produce the fruit of the Spirit.

Does the Holy Spirit or the flesh habitually dominate your mind? You will know by what your life is producing. Set your mind on the flesh and you will produce flesh. Let it be under the power and control of the Holy Spirit and you will become like Jesus Christ in your behavior.

The only way not to walk in the flesh is to change masters of the mind. "Be transformed by the renewing of the mind" (Romans 12:2). When we set our minds on the Spirit, we produce spiritual things that are pleasing to God. The Amplified Bible reads, "For those who are according to the flesh and controlled by its unholy desires, set their minds on and pursue those things which gratify the flesh. But those who are according to the Spirit, set their minds on and seek those things which gratify the Holy Spirit.

Where do you choose to let your thoughts dwell? You are what you think. Will you not now choose to bow your mind to the control of the Spirit of God? Let Him control your thinking. Let the desire of your heart be to depend not upon yourself, but on Christ alone. That is the work of the Holy Spirit within you. We have everything we need to live the Christian life in Him, and what He chooses to provide. Our inner resource is God Himself, the Holy Spirit. Let Him control your mind, your heart, and your actions will be pleasing to God.

Chapter Twenty: God's Purpose and Plans for You

Many people go through life feeling discouraged about themselves and thinking they do not have a plan or a purpose in life. But that is not true. Whoever you are, in any event of your life experience, talents, physical ability, or role, you have a purpose.

Ephesians 2:10 states, "For we are God's workmanship, created in Christ Jesus to do good works, which God prepared in advance for us to do."

Look at the two points in this verse:

1. God created you. You are not an accident.

2. God has a plan for you. You have a purpose in life.

You are designed to know God

One purpose in life is to draw close to God. You do this through Jesus Christ.

"I am the bread of life" (John 6:35).

"I am the way and the truth and the life. No one comes to the Father except through me"

(John 14:6).

"If you confess with your mouth, 'Jesus is Lord,' and believe in your heart that God raised him

from the dead, you will be saved. For it is with the heart that you believe and are justified,

and it is with your mouth that you confess and are saved" (Romans 10:9-10).

You are designed for God's glory

One purpose in life is to glorify God in this world.

"Bring my sons from afar and my daughters from the ends of the earth, everyone who is called

by my name, whom I created for my glory, whom I formed and made" (Isaiah 43:6-7).

You are designed to praise God

One purpose in life is to praise and worship God.

"All the nations you have made will come and worship before you, O Lord; They will

bring glory to your name" (Psalm 86:9).

"I will praise you, O Lord my God, with all my heart, I will glorify your name forever"

(Psalm 86:12).

You are designed to grow in the fruit of the Spirit

One purpose in life is to develop in character. The type of person you become is more

important than your success and failures in the world.

"But the fruit of the Spirit is love, joy, peace, patience, kindness, goodness, faithfulness,

gentleness and self-control" (Galatians 5:22-23).

You are designed to spread the gospel

One purpose in life is to tell others about Jesus' love for them.

"Declare his glory among the nations, his marvelous deeds among all peoples" (Psalm 96:3).

"Make known among the nations what he has done and proclaim that his name is exalted" (Isaiah 12:4).

"Therefore go and make disciples of all nations, baptizing them in the name of the Father, and of the Son, and of the Holy Spirit, and teaching them to obey everything I have commandedyou" (Matthew 28:19-20).

You are designed to use the talents God gave you

One purpose in life is to develop your gifts.

"Just as each of us has one body with many members, and these members do not all have the

[164]

same function, so in Christ we who are many form one body, and each member belongs to all

the others. We have different gifts, according to the grace given us. If a man's gift is

prophesying, let him use it in proportion to his faith. If it is serving, let him serve; if it is

teaching, let him teach; if it is encouraging, let him encourage; if it is contributing to the

needs of others, let him give generously; if it is leadership, let him govern diligently; if it is

showing mercy, let him do it cheerfully" (Romans 12:4-8).

Do not minimize your role.

- Live life as an adventurer.

All Christians collectively form the body of Christ. The body is formed of many different parts (Romans 12:48 and 1 Corinthians 12:12-27). All are important. It does not matter what part of the body you are.

"On the contrary, those parts of the body that seem to be weaker or indispensible, and the parts that we think are less honorable we treat with special honor. And the parts that are un-presentable are treated with special modesty, while our presentable parts need no special treatment. But God has combined the members of the body and has given greater honor to the parts that lacked it"

(1 Corinthians 12:22-24).

- Overcome jealousy or bitterness.

Do not be upset if you do not have a place of prominence, for as you read in the above verses, God gives special honor to people with "less honorable" roles.

- Do not downplay the value of what you do.

Do not compare yourself to others or give up if someone seems to do a better job than you. Of course, there are others who have more talent. If all the evangelists or witnesses or teachers in the world decided to stop trying because someone else did a better job, where would we be? What counts is that you be faithful. God gave you talents and abilities. He expects you to develop them.

What God has prepared for you

The Scripture shows us that God has arranged for every Christian a life that is filled with joy. This life is totally at peace, and has no walls in its fellowship with God, and is not contrary to His will in any way. The life that God has arranged for a Christian is one that does not thirst after the world. It walks apart from sin, and is victorious over sin. It is holy, powerful and victorious. It knows the will of God and fellowships with God without interruptions. This is the life that God prepared in the Bible for a Christian.

[166]

God has arranged a life that is hidden with Christ in God. What can touch this life? What can affect or shake this life? Just as Christ is unshakable, we also are unshakable. Just as He is transcendent over all things, we also are transcendent over all things. Our standing before God is the same as Christ's standing before God. We should never consider that we are destined for weakness and failure. There is no room for such a thought for a Christian in the Bible. Colossians 3:4 says, "Christ our life." Christ is far above everything. Nothing can touch Him. Glory! This is the life of Christ!

The life that God prepared for a Christian is one that is filled with peace and joy. It is a life that is full of activity, energy, and God's will. But what kind of life do we live? If we are not living the life that God has ordained, we need to overcome and breakthrough in this situation. Consequently, we need to consider our experience today. This is not an easy subject to speak on. Some of our experiences may be quite sad. However, we will see our lack when we humble ourselves. Only then will God grant us the grace we need.

This life is a gift, not a reward

Please remember that victory is a gift; it is not a reward. What is a gift? A gift is a present; it is something freely given. What we receive as a result of work is a reward. But what we freely receive without doing any work is a gift. The latter is given to us freely; it has nothing to do with what we have done, and we do not have to utilize any effort to get it. The former receives our work; we must strive for it before we can have it. He is overcoming life which we speak of does not require our own effort. We can read 1 Corinthians 15:57, which says, "But thanks be to God who gives us the victory

[167]

through our Lord Jesus Christ." Victory is something that God has prepared and given us. Our victory comes to us free of charge; we do not have to earn it by our own strength.

Chapter Twenty-one: God's Restoration

God is finally and personally mindful of you. He sees you, and He desires you to "understand that you know" that He has not deserted or rejected you (Hebrew 13:5). He desires you to know that at all times, specifically in the dark of night in your soul, He is still with you and He is the Exceptional Restorer. Notice what God said through the prophet Joel, "So I will restore to you the years that the swarming locust has eaten..." (Joel 2:25a). God loves to restore what has been consumed in our lives. That's His area of expertise.

Joel chronicles or transcribes God's word of hope, "Fair not, O land; be glad and rejoice, for the Lord has done marvelous things!" (v. 21). God speaks concerning the abundance, stressing the process of renewal and the release of the latter rain and the spring rain (v. 23). There would be harvest and fruitfulness again (v. 22). The vats would overflow with new wine (v. 24). He says, "I am not just going to fill your vats again, your vats are going to overflow! Your barn walls are going to bust down!" That is what God does. Scripturally, that's what restoration looks like.

God restores by increase and multiplication

I have come to understand that when God restores, He delivers an increase. When He restores, He multiplies. There is something about the restoring character of God. During the process of restoration, God delivers the object of restoration back in a much better way than it was in its previous state and

[169]

He increases it and multiplies it. He forever likes to add more. Check out Job. When God restored Job, He gave unto Job, double (Job 42:10). That is just the character of God.

In the Word, we see that if loss came to someone or something was stolen, that God would decree that the return be greater than what was robbed or plundered. Once in the blue moon, would the return be "one for one." Just about every single time, the return was directed to be more than that, a double blessing or four or five times greater (Exodus 22:1; 22:4; Leviticus 6:5, 22:14). And it did not stop there! There was a "sevenfold" rule in connection with restoration (included vengeance) as well. Proverb 6:31b says, "Yet when he (the thief) is found, he must restore sevenfold..."

Today, I trust that God installs it like this in the spirit. When the thief steals, he must give back sevenfold. When the adversary comes to kill, steal, and destroy, God has arranged forever in eternity that you must get back sevenfold. And God will restore you in a much better way than you were at the beginning, and then He will increase and multiply what was stolen. That is our God because God is good! Pay attention. We need this revelation.

For instance, when God desires to restore your anointing, it honors Him that you make a statement like the following: "God desires to give me a double portion of anointing!" When God restores, you are going to have double joy, everlasting joy, a double share. He is going to bless you with an increase and demand the thief to give back sevenfold.

If your marriage needs to be restored then stir up your faith and ask, "My God, please, I want You to restore my marriage, and I want it to be double the intimacy." Get bold. Don't just settle for an "okay, restore my marriage" attitude. "Restore my marriage and give it to me double."

"Restore my finances and give it to me double."

Restore my anointing and give it to me double."

We can ask God because of the character of the restoration process of the Holy Spirit. He increases, and He multiplies.

For example, when God heals my body, when God restores my body, I am not just going to be healthy, I am going to have divine health. And then I am going to be able to minister healing to the sick, because I am getting a healing anointing in the process. That is restoration.

Take notice to this, anyone that gives up houses, lands brothers, sisters, possessions in this lifetime for the sake of the gospel, God will restore back one hundredfold now, (Mark 10:29-30). The Lord does abundantly above what you can ask. He does abundantly above what you can think of, (Ephesians 3:20). We need to have a larger vision. When we stand in faith and believe that God is enormously enthusiastic about wanting to declare restoration into our lives, we truly honor Him.

God's purpose in restoration

God desires you to know that He is anxiously interested in achieving personal restoration in your life. His wish is that when you experience the blessing of personal restoration, (so have faith), you will be blessed, but even more, that you will draw nearer and nearer into His heart. His main purpose for

[171]

restoration is intimacy with you. Do you understand that without you, without your love and friendship, God is grieved? Focus on that.

You understand restoration is something supernatural. After Jesus died on the cross for you and me and we received Him as our Lord and Savior, He restored each one of us into personal relationship and fellowship with Him by taking our sins upon Himself and drawing us into His heart. It is like we are restored in such a manner that we experience what Adam and Eve had with God when He walked with them in the garden, is also our experience to enjoy. His presence is the garden. Such restoration recovers, and it goes beyond time, space, and eternity. And this blessing is accessible for us today. What an essential revelation to have. Yet, the choice is ours.

Notice! We can chose to stand in faith trusting that God desires to restore to us the same kind of special intimacy that He engaged with Adam and Eve in the Garden of Eden. I do not believe that we have to wait for the day when we die and go to heaven to enjoy such relationship with God because "the kingdom of Heaven is within you" (Luke 17:21). From what I notice in Scripture Heaven for me began the day that I received eternal life. That is Heaven.

We are the bride of Christ, whether we stand before the Father individually as His son or daughter, or corporately as the body of Christ. I wish us to be an excited bride, expecting the union, the oneness, and the intimacy that is saved for us to take enjoyment in, in Christ, with the Father. He wants to speak to us clearly as a friend speaks to a friend (Exodus 33:11; John 15:12-15). To want the presence of the Father above everything else, and in a much greater way than our common thinking and rules, this brings the Father such great pleasure.

Let us not let man's tradition, or whatever denomination you were raised in, set limits for what you can or cannot accept from the hand of the Lord. There remains a rest in Him. Unbelief has kept us from walking in the full inheritance of all that we can have in the spirit.

I desire you to get hungry for the Father; be more centered on being hungry for the manifestation of the glory of God, union and intimacy. Notice! God opened the garden again. He said to come boldly before the throne (Hebrews 4:16). He tear opened the veil (Luke 23:45). We can enter "the most Holy Place by the blood of Jesus, by a new and living way which He consecrated for us, through the veil, that is His flesh..." (Hebrews 10:19-20).

God do not want you to lose hope!

Read Genesis 3:22-24 the story about the Garden of Eden and say, "That belongs to me! There is nobody but me keeping me from that place. Because of the shed blood of Jesus Christ, I can enter." Adam and Eve lost entrance to the garden because of their disobedience to God, but Jesus has set us free from the law of sin and death by His shed blood (Romans 8:1-2) and we are no longer hindered from the place of intimacy with God the Father in the garden. Don't lose the hope Jesus provided.

Pay attention. Today, God is going to release and restore hope to you. So why not prepare your heart right now for what God desires to do in your life? We hardly began this

[173]

year, the year of restoration, new beginnings, and intimacy with God.

God is not going to let you down, and He desires your heart to embrace hope once again, the restoration of hope. Allow such knowledge become a healing balm to your heart while you think about Paul's encouraging message to the Romans.

"Therefore, having been justified by faith, we have peace with God through our Lord Jesus Christ, and through whom also we have access by faith into this grace in which we stand and rejoice in hope of the glory of God. And not only that , but we also glory in tribulations, knowing that tribulation produces perseverance, and perseverance, character, and character, hope. Now hope does not disappoint, because the love of God has been poured out in our hearts by the Holy Spirit who was given to us" (Romans 5:1-5).

Restoration is similar to a two-edged sword

So, restoration is similar to a two-edged sword. One sharp edge reveals our own personal restoration victories and the other edge cuts off the plans of the enemy over other people's lives. What a double blessing!

Therefore, we need to recall that during the process of restoration, there is always a divine test. Before Joseph regained freedom, and he took the throne in Egypt (second only to Pharaoh) he was taken into a huge God-ordained season of testing (Genesis 37-50. Psalms 105:19 says, "Until the time that his word came to pass, the word of the Lord tested him." Joseph had the prophetic word of the Lord, but until it actually came to pass, this word tested him.

Likewise, many of you have the prophetic word of the Lord concerning areas of restoration coming upon your lives; however, today, the fulfillment has not manifested, it's still on its way. Stand your ground in the time of testing, the time of waiting. God will surely come and bring restoration precisely at the perfect moment.

Pay attention. I hold that God is going to stir up the gifts of the Spirit in your life. God is going to restore your vision and your purpose. For some of you, He is going to restore your marriage. Some of you today will experience God restoring your finances and giving you jubilee and supernatural cancellation of your debt.

Repeat, "God, I want you to restore my soul. Anoint my head with fresh oil." The anointing is going to restore your soul, your mind, your will and your emotions.

See Yourself How God Sees You

Much of your joy in life hinges on how you think God sees you.

Unfortunately, many of us have a wrong idea of God's opinion of us. We base it on what we have been taught, our bad experiences in life, and many other beliefs. We may think God is disappointed in us or that we will never measure up. We may even believe God is angry with us because we cannot stop sinning.

But if we want to know the naked truth , we need to go to the source: God himself.

God says to you how He sees you in His personal message to His followers, the Bible. What you can learn in those pages about your relationship with Him is nothing short of fascinating.

God Sees You as His Beloved Child

If you are a born-again believer, you are not a stranger to God. You are not a castaway, although you may sometimes feel alone. The heavenly Father loves you and sees you as one of His children:

"I will be a Father to you, and you will be my sons and daughters, says the Lord Almighty."

(2 Corinthian 6:17-18)

"How great is the love the Father has lavished on us, that we should be called children of God! and that is what we are!" (1 John 3:1)

No matter how old you are, it's comforting to know that you are a child of God, the great I Am! You belong to a loving, protective Father. God, who is everywhere, keeps watch over you and is always ready to listen when you want to talk with Him.

But the privileges do not stop there. Since you have been adopted into the family, you have the same rights as Jesus:

"Now if we are children, then we are heirs, heirs of God and joint heirs with Christ, if truly we share in his suffering in order that we may also share in his glory." (Romans 8:17)

God Sees You as Forgiven

Many Believers are struggling under a heavy load of regret, afraid they have disappointed God, but if you know

[176]

Jesus as Savior, God sees you as forgiven. He does not hold your past sins against you.

The Scriptures are clear on this point. God sees you as righteous because the death of Jesus cleansed you from your sins.

"You are forgiving and good, O Lord, abounding in love to all who call to you." (Psalm 86:5)

"All the prophets testify about him that everyone who believes in him receives forgiveness of sins through his name." (Acts 10:43)

You do not have to worry about being holy enough, because Jesus was perfectly holy when he went to the cross on your behalf. God sees you as forgiven. Your job is to accept that gift.

God Sees You as Saved

At times you may doubt your salvation, but as a child of God and a member of His family, God sees you as saved. Continually, in the Bible, God reassures Christians of our true condition:

"All men will hate you because of me, but he who stands firm to the end will be saved." (Matthew 10:22)

"And everyone who calls on the name of the Lord will be saved." (Acts 2:21)

"For God did not appoint us to suffer wrath but to receive salvation through our Lord Jesus Christ." (1 Thessalonians 5:9)

[177]

You do not have to speculate. You do not have to labor and attempt to earn your salvation by works. To know God considers you saved is fantastically reassuring. You can live in joy because Jesus paid the penalty for your sins so you can spend eternity with God in heaven.

God Sees You as Having Hope

When misfortune hits and you feel as if life is closing in on you, God sees you as a person of hope. No matter how desolate the situation, Jesus is with you through it all.

Hope is not depended on what we can gather up. It is depended on the One we have hope in, Almighty God. If your hope feels weak, recall, child of God, your heavenly Father is strong. When you keep your attention focused on Him, you will have hope.

"For I know the plans I have for you, declares the Lord, plans to prosper you and not to harm you, plans to give hope and a future." (Jeremiah 29:11)

God made you, loves you, and desires to be involve in your life on an everyday bases. Holding on to that truth, can at times be difficult. As you search to experience God working in your life, you must first learn to see yourself as God sees you.

Five key principles influence self-perception

As you start to utilize these principles to your life, you will be able to adopt God's perception of you as His child. When we accept our identity as a child of God, anything is possible.

1. Before you can comprehend who you really are, you must first comprehend how to correctly judge reality.

[178]

People explain reality in many ways: if I can see it, it's real; if I can experience it, it's real; if science can prove its existence, it's real; and for some people, if God says it's real, it's real. So which reality is dependable?

"If I can see it, it's real."

There are moments when this statement is true, and yet, gravity, airwaves, and odorless gases such as oxygen or even carbon monoxide are examples of things that are very real, but that we cannot see.

"If I can experience it, it's real."

Here again, experience can be real, but we know that optical illusions, visions, and holograms are all very real experiences, but in fact are not reality.

"If science can prove its existence, it's real."

Science is frequently a very good indicator of reality, but it too can change over time. Malaria has killed masses of people than all the wars put together. The word malaria means "bad air" which medical science believed was the reason for the disease. It wasn't until the beginning of the 20th century that mosquitoes were identified as the real cause for the spread of the disease. Scientists are constantly making new discoveries which many times reveal errors in what they had previously believed to be true. There are hindrances to our knowledge and understanding of science.

Well, what about the conviction that if God says its real, it's real? If God through His Word tells us something is true but we can't see it, experience it, or scientifically prove it, can it be true?

[179]

One of the main truths about trusting God is that when God says something is true, then it's true. He knows all things. His righteous nature does not allow Him to lie. With every passing day history continues to prove the absolute accuracy of what God has stated in the Bible. What God says is absolutely true even when we are not able to understand it with our limited reasoning.

There are three realms of existence that are involved in the area of life. We are very aware of the visible, physical realm which we experience through our senses. This includes the things that we can see, hear, taste, touch and smell.

But we are also very dependent on the invisible, physical realm which includes things like molecules, bacteria, and gases.

We are not aware of these things through our natural senses. Only through recent scientific technology have we begun to understand how changes in this invisible realm affect our physical well being.

Both the visible and invisible dimensions of the physical realm exist within the larger context of the spirit realm. This is the realm within which God and angels exist. It is every bit as real as the physical realm even though we are not naturally conscious of its existence. We must stand on the reality of who God is and what He tells us in His Word, the Bible.

2.   Realities in the physical realm are influenced by life in the spiritual realm.

"So we fix our eyes not on what is seen, but on what is unseen. For what is seen is temporary, but what is unseen is eternal." (2 Corinthians 4:18)

The physical realm in this verse is "what is seen" and "temporary." It is what we see naturally through our senses, experiences and scientific knowledge. The spiritual realm is identified by the words "what is unseen" and "eternal" or permanent.

Paul is not saying to us to deny physical realities. He is saying that as a matter of priority those things that happen in the spiritual realm are more essential than what happens in the physical realm. Activity in the spiritual realm has a considerable effect on what takes place in the physical realm. God wants us to be aware of this principle and to focus our attention on spiritual realities. The spiritual reality for each one of us is that God see each person as one of His unique creations.

3. Spiritual birth (being born again) is an essential to having an identity in Christ.

Jesus declared, "I tell you the truth, no one can see the kingdom of God unless he is born again. "How can a man be born when he is old? Nicodemus asked. Surely he cannot enter a second time into his mother's womb to be born!" Jesus answered, "I tell you the truth, no man can enter the kingdom of God unless he is born of water and Spirit. Flesh gives birth to flesh, but the Spirit gives birth to spirit. You should not be surprised at my saying, "You must be born again." (John 3:3-7)

Our parents gave us a physical birth, and it is the Holy Spirit that gives us spiritual birth.

Death came into the world because of what one man (Adam) did and it is because of what this other man (Christ) has done that now there is the resurrection from the dead. Everyone dies because all of us are related to Adam, being members of his sinful race and wherever there is sin, death happens. But all who are related to Christ will rise again. (1 Corinthians 15:21-22)

Life must be restored to our spirit before it is possible to know the Father, understand His truth, and develop an intimate relationship with Him. When we welcome Christ into our life as Savior and Lord, we begin our new identity in Christ. This is a key element in seeing ourselves as God sees us.

4.   Spiritual birth happens in a total transformation of our being. We become a new creation.

Our soul has been programmed by our inherited "old sin nature." We were born with a natural attraction for false beliefs and wrong values. We have grown up in an atmosphere that penetrates our mind with deception and rewards wrong behavior. This kind of mindset is natural to us because it is all that we have ever known.

However, the Bible informs us in 2 Corinthians 5:17, "Therefore, if anyone is in Christ, he is a new creation, the old has gone, the new has come!"

When we receive Christ into our life, our soul is programmed by the Holy Spirit through our new nature. This is achieved by renewing our minds with God's truth and rejecting our old false beliefs.

The problem we all face is: Why are there two conflicting influences if now only the new nature lives?

The answer is in comprehending that our new nature has been set up to control our soul, but we are not familiar with it. It is alive and ready for action but goes unnoticed because of our ignorance. The old nature has died and no longer has the power to control our soul. But, we still have the thought patterns, memories, emotional responses and habit patterns from the past which it created. We continue to acknowledge the old nature and live according to the patterns it previously set up because that's all we have ever known. But, the new nature illustrates who we are now, and we continually develop into it. We truly are new creations in Christ!

5. By faith you must receive God's forgiveness to us through the death of Christ on the cross for our sins. Christ makes it obtainable for us to have a relationship with the Father.

We must grasp what God says in His Word about who we now are in Christ and believe Him. We need to inform ourselves that God's portrayal of us is now a reality, in any event of how we feel, or have perceived ourselves, or how others view us.

Your new relationship with the Father means you are His child and co-heir with Jesus His son! You have a brand new nature and God is continually working in your life through the power of His Holy Spirit!!!

Conclusion
Do Not Be Afraid To Begin Again

More often than not, it is not the criticism of strangers but the rejection of those closest to us that causes us the most pain and damage. In fact, I maintain rejection causes some of the most painful bondage that anyone ever encounters because it affects what you and I believe about ourselves. This is what takes place: when a person or group of people, who may have been trying to hurt or control us, judges us unlovable, unfit, or worthless, we subconsciously accept that others must hold the same belief.

We may not discern its effects. We may not think it bothers us. We may not even realize or remember that we were rejected. But when we are made to feel that we are unwanted, unloved, or unworthy of respect, we are wounded deep within our souls in a way that sharply affects how we view ourselves, others, and God. Naturally, we become more self-critical and begin to look for ways others may reinforce the negative thoughts we have about ourselves, at times even arousing people to reject us by acting out.

This is because rejection strikes at the foundation of our identity, altering what we think is true about who we are and what we are worth. Why? Because of the sinful nature within us. Remember, "sin reigned death" (Romans 5:21). The end goal of the sin nature is destruction (Romans 5:12), so it is understandable that the harmful messages we hear find fertile soil in our hearts and take root. This is why it is much easier to believe the hurtful things said about us than comments that

[184]

encourage or edify us. We hug the messages that hurry us along the path to destruction (Psalm 16:25) and dismiss that which reminds us we are created in the image of God (Genesis 1:26).

And the truth of the matter, if we fail to identify the presence of rejection in our lives and deal with it, it will continue to cause us pain and spoil every relationship we have. Therefore, we must root out every false message of being unloved, unwanted, and unworthy that has been implanted in our lives and replace it with the truth of Scripture (Psalm 107:20).

The only way to have victory over rejection is to release the harmful ideas we have about ourselves and take hold of God's truth.

Beloved there is only one person who knows your true worth and value, and that is the One who knit you together in your mother's womb (Psalm 139:13-16). Only He knows what is in your heart and what is possible for your future (1Samuel 16:7; Jeremiah 29:11). Only He is worthy of judging your value and can set you free from the false messages that keep you in bondage (Hebrews 4:12-13). That one is the triune God, who loves you without measure, the Father who created you, the Lord Jesus who saves you, and the Holy Spirit who indwells you (1 Peter 1:1-2).

The Lord is inviting you into a deeper relationship with Him. This place of intimacy is where you will experience new levels of His glory. As you enter into this place of rest, you will develop the fellowship with the Father that you have longed for. This is the place where He will visit you. This is the place where visions will be received and His voice will be heard. It is the place where His anointing is released and you will encounter Him in a new and greater way. This fellowship with Him is the place where revelation is deposited. His gifts are cultivated and His Word will come alive. This is the place that brings refreshing to your soul. It is a place where you can escape out of business and the distractions of the world. This is one of the mysteries of the kingdom, to live in God and Jesus in you.

Do not be afraid to begin again. Whether it was your choice or it was determined for you... your best days are ahead of you. Whatever you at one time felt or experienced can be enormously overshadowed by what is ahead. You have to just move forward to see. I am thrilled for you. Please do not be afraid. Walk by faith, not by sight and see God do the impossible!

Ecclesiastes 7:8, "Better is the end of a thing than the beginning thereof: and the patient in spirit is better than the proud in spirit."

Scriptural Affirmations

The Scriptural affirmations below will help you renew your mind.

1. I can do all things through Christ which strengthens me.

2. God is able to make every favor and earthly blessing come to me in abundance, so that in all things

    at all times, having all that I need, I will abound in every good work (Corinthians 9:8).

3. I am a child of God and have overcome my poverty, sickness and disease, because Greater is He who

    lives in me than He who lives in the world (John 4:4).

4. Glory be to God! By His mighty power at work within me, He is able to do exceedingly and

    over-abundantly, beyond anything I could ask, think or pray (Ephesians 3:20).

5. My God will make a way where there is no way for God is able. Nothing is impossible with Him

because of my faith. My healing has been signed, sealed and delivered, glory be to God, praise

the Lord, Hallelujah!!! Thank you Jesus.

6. I recognize Jesus Christ as the Messiah, the Word who became flesh and dwelt among us. I

believe that He came to destroy the works of Satan, that He disarmed the rulers and authorities,

having triumphed over them (John 1:1, 14; Colossians 2:15; 1 John 3:8).

7. I believe that I am a child of God. I believe that I was saved by the grace of God through faith, that it

was a gift and not the result of any works on my part (Ephesians 2:8; 1 John 3:1-3).

8. I recognize that there is only one true and living God, who exists as the Father, Son and Holy Spirit,

and that He is worthy of all honor, praise and worship as the Creator, Sustainer, Beginning and End

of all things (Exodus 20:2, 3; Revelation 4:11; 5:9, 10; Isaiah 43:1, 7, 21).

9. I refuse to fear; I will not be dismayed for God is with me. I am strengthened by His might, yes, God

is my helper. He is upholding me with the right hand of His righteousness, for His Name sake

(Isaiah 41:10).

[188]

10. Though I walk in the midst of trouble, You will revive me; You will stretch forth Your hand against

the wrath of my enemies, and Your right hand will save me (Psalm 138:7).

11. I will be glad and rejoice in Your mercy and steadfast love, because You have seen my affliction,

You have taken note of my life's distresses (Psalm 31:7).

12. I will wait upon the LORD while He is renewing my strength; I am mounting up with wings like an

eagle; I am running the race, and I am not weary; I am walking the walk and I do not feel faint. I

waited patiently for the LORD; and He inclined His ear unto me, and He heard my cry (Isaiah 40:31;

Psalm 40:1).

13. God said that I will prosper and be in health, even as my soul prosper, and I am prospering and I am

healthy in mind, body, soul and spirit (3 John 1:2).

14. Jesus Christ bore my sins in His body on the tree, so I, who have died to sin, am now living for

rectitude; by His wounds I am healed (1 Peter 2:24).

15. I believe that He delivered me out of the domain of darkness and transferred me into His kingdom

of love, and in Him I have redemption, and the forgiveness of sins and I am grateful (Colossians 1:13-14).

16. I believe that I was saved by the grace of God through faith, that it was a gift and not the result of any works on my part.

17. I resolve to stand firm in my faith and resist the evil one. The Lord, inscribes on my heart the truth

of who He is and what He has done to secure my eternal salvation.

18. Blessed be the God and Father of my Lord Jesus Christ. Who according to His abundant mercy has

begotten me again to a living hope through the resurrection of Jesus Christ from the dead and into

an inheritance incorruptible and undefiled and that does not fade away, that which is reserved in

heaven for me. Who is kept by the power of God through faith for salvation ready to be revealed in

the last time.

Final Prayer

Father, how appreciative I am that You know when I feel discouraged and utterly lost. I give thanks for Your kindness toward me and Your longing to heal my bruises. You know, Lord, how easy it is for me to become disheartened - even over the very trials You send to restore my damaged state of mind. So Father, whenever I feel desolation rising up within me, help me to remember to come before You in prayer and seek Your loving face. Prompt me to renew my dedication to Your plans for my future and zero in on Your matchless character. Help me to embrace who You have created me to be and may Your praises forever be on my lips.

Lord, honestly You are good - the holy, sovereign, and trustworthy God of all that exists. You are adorned with majesty and strength - Your wisdom none can grasp. Your unlimited love and mind-boggling grace make my heart rejoice.

Thank You, Father, for giving me hope. Even when everything around me seems to be against me and there is no rescue in sight, I know You are working on my behalf in the unseen. Honestly, Your great and mighty plans are higher and beyond all I could possibly ask or conceive. So help me be a temple of your glory - leading others to know You and helping them to find healing in Your unfailing presence.

Thank You, Father, for giving me the victory over hopelessness and for making it the classroom of learning where I can draw closer to You. In Jesus' precious name, I pray. Amen.

[191]

About the Author

Dr. Yolanda Webster is passionate to see individuals deepen their intimacy with God and experience a fulfilling life both now and for eternity. She was born and raised in Brooklyn possessing a wonderful heritage, Caribbean and Southern decent. She has been married for 41 years, has five children, seven grandchildren and now resides in Long Island.

Dr. Webster graduated with a doctoral degree from Columbia University, Teachers College. She served as a teacher for the Board of Education for many years in the area of music education. She taught on both elementary and secondary levels.

Dr. Webster has served as a member of New Life Cathedral Church in Brooklyn for over 30 years under the founder and senior pastor Bishop Robert J. Rochford in the area of Ministry of Help.

Dr. Webster is the author of "Weeping May Endure for a Night, But Joy Comes in the Morning," and "The Modern Day Wilderness Experience."

Dr. Webster Also served as a secretary for H.O.P.E. (How Our People Exist) Organization for several years under the late Carl McCallister ministering to dialysis patients, and she is presently a member of Brooklyn Kidney Club of Downstate for people with kidney disease, a center for community health promotion and wellness.

Other Books by
Dr. Yolanda Webster

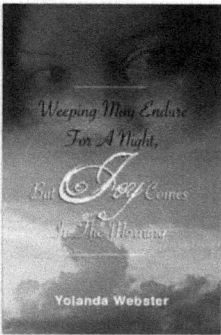

Weeping may Endure for the Night but Joy Comes in the Morning

"Weeping May Endure For A Night", is about a Christian female who is stricken with a deadly disease. Despite many attempts of praying for healing, she does not recover. She learns to live with the illness. She passes from death to life through a metamorphosis of her faith in God. As this process takes place, she makes it through the night to the next morning. The night represents suffering, pain, and death, while the day represents healing, recovery, and rebirth.

This book is for you if you have no hope. It's for you if you bought the lie that you lack faith because you did not receive your healing. That's not true. God is the source of your faith.

Your existence is bigger than any circumstance, situation, problem or test you may face.

Inside these pages lie solutions to developing a true relationship with God. You will not necessarily become immune to trouble, but you will attain a life that is fulfilling, meaningful and more fruitful than you ever thought possible.

By applying the solutions in this book, the author rose from her tough life to one of amazing accomplishments. She learned that she had untapped ability, she learned how to release it. To find out more about this inspiring book visit...
www.DiscoverDiamondBooks.com

The Modern Day Wilderness Experience

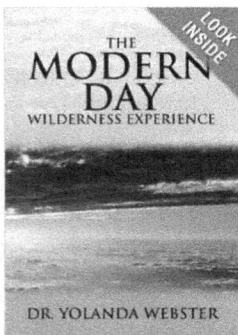

The Modern Day Wilderness Experience chronicles the author's painful ordeals of rejection from the system during her career with the Board of Education, linking it to biblical accounts of wilderness experiences. Anyone who has been the victim of rejection, verbal abuse or harassment can identify with her struggles to be accepted as she speaks straight from the heart.

Her honesty tugs at the reader's emotions. She relates how traumatic experiences can be used for good and how a Christian can actually grow through hurtful encounters with others. Buy the complete printed version of this inspiring, encouraging, and enlighting Book by visiting www.DiscoverDiamondBooks.com

Diamond Enterprises
"Rise and Shine with Priceless Inspiration"

www.ingramcontent.com/pod-product-compliance
Lightning Source LLC
Chambersburg PA
CBHW072003090426
42740CB00011B/2066